THE LAKE DISTRICT

NATIONAL PARK

John Wyatt

Webb & Bower
MICHAEL JOSEPH

Acknowledgements

Thanks are due to the following for their assistance in the preparation of this guide-book: Tom Clare, Archaeologist, Cumbria County Council; Graham Coggins, Countryside Commission, Northern Region; David Hawkes, Forestry Commission, Grizedale Forest; Nigel Sale, National Trust, North West Regional Office; Miss Vicky Slowe, Abbot Hall Art Gallery, Kendal; and the staff of the Lake District National Park Authority.

New photographs were taken for the Countryside Commission by Mike Williams and Geoffrey Berry. Other material has been used with permission from the following sources: Abbot Hall Art Gallery, Kendal, page 63; Geoffrey Berry, pages 23, 27, 34, 52, 53, 56, 71, 83, 85; The Dove Cottage Trust, pages 74; *Punch*, page 13; Royal Society for the Protection of Birds, pages 92, 98; Tate Gallery, page 75; and Barry Tullett, page 67.

First published in Great Britain 1987 by
Webb & Bower (Publishers) Limited
9 Colleton Crescent, Exeter, Devon EX2 4BY
in association with Michael Joseph Limited
27 Wright's Lane, London W8 5SL
and The Countryside Commission,
John Dower House, Crescent Place,
Cheltenham, Glos GL50 3RA

Designed by Ron Pickless

Production by Nick Facer/Rob Kendrew

Illustrations by Rosamund Gendle/Ralph Stobart

Text and new photographs Copyright © The Countryside Commission
Illustrations Copyright © Webb & Bower (Publishers) Ltd

British Library Cataloguing in Publication Data
The National parks of Britain.
The Lake District
1. National parks and reserves — England —
Guide-books 2. England — Description and
travel — 1971– — Guide-books.
I. Wyatt, John, *1925–*
914.2′04858 SB484.G7.

ISBN 0–86350–133–8

Typeset in Great Britain by Keyspools Ltd., Golborne, Lancs.

Printed and bound in Hong Kong by Mandarin Offset.

Contents

Preface

The Lake District is one of ten national parks which were established in the 1950s. These largely upland and coastal areas represent the finest landscapes in England and Wales and present us all with opportunities to savour breathtaking scenery, to take part in invigorating outdoor activities, to experience rural community life, and most importantly, to relax in peaceful surroundings.

The designation of national parks is the product of those who had the vision, more than fifty years ago, to see that ways were found to ensure that the best of our countryside should be recognized and protected, that the way of life therein should be sustained, and that public access for open-air recreation should be encouraged.

As the government planned Britain's post-war reconstruction, John Dower, architect, rambler and national park enthusiast, was asked to report on how the national park ideal adopted in other countries could work for England and Wales. An important consideration was the ownership of land within the parks. Unlike other countries where large tracts of land are in public ownership, and thus national parks can be owned by the nation, here in Britain most of the land within the national parks was, and still is, privately owned. John Dower's report was published in 1945 and its recommendations accepted. Two years later another report drafted by a committee chaired by Sir Arthur Hobhouse proposed an administrative system for the parks, and this was embodied in the National Parks and Access to the Countryside Act 1949.

This Act set up the National Parks Commission to designate national parks and advise on their administration. In 1968 this became the Countryside Commission but we continue to have national responsibility for our parks which are administered by local government, either through committees of the county councils or independent planning boards.

This guide to the landscape, settlements and natural history of the Lake District National Park is one of a series on all ten parks. As well as helping the visitor appreciate the park and its attractions, the guides outline the achievements and pressures facing the national park authorities today.

Our national parks are a vital asset, and we all have a duty to care for and conserve them. Learning about the parks and their value to us all is a crucial step in creating more awareness of the importance of the national parks so that each of us can play our part in seeing that they are protected for all to enjoy.

Sir Derek Barber
Chairman
Countryside Commission

Introduction

'The Lake District': the name of this sublime area of English countryside evokes blissful memories to the many who have fallen under its spell, and no doubt an agreeable picture of countryside pleasures to many who have yet to savour it. As long ago as the sixteenth century Camden, the Elizabethan historian, was acclaiming the landscape of mountains and lakes: '. . . for the variety thereof it smileth upon the beholders and giveth contentment to as many as travaile it'.

The 'variety thereof' is the overwhelming attraction. Crammed into this favoured north-west corner of England is so very much that is uniquely beautiful; and much that is the best of British landscape. There are the rugged mountains, modest in size by Alpine standards, but managing by some subtle sorcery of scale to suggest magnitude: their radiating ridges, their riven sides, and spilling waters, long green dales, hills and some sixteen lakes, with rivers, woods and forests; pastures latticed with drystone walls; and small settlements.

Typically the scene is the classic one of extreme contrasts: the buttressed walls and gables of hills and fierce crags, towering above the still waters and green fields of the floor. Calm tranquillity at the foot of a petrified cataclysm. But if the ancient earth movements and climatic catastrophes cast up, forged and carved the general shape of the scene, the colour and texture owe much to the centuries of human settlement. Here the hill farmer, faced with the stern discipline of the uncompromising land structure, the lean earth, the uncertain climate, has had to respond in sympathy, not in conflict, with his environment. The physical effect is an essential ingredient of the alchemy which gives all a haunting atmospheric appeal. A feeling of wholeness greater than the sum of its parts, a harmony, a happy balance.

But that is not all, for the scene changes at every turn of the way. And each set-piece is never the same. Falling water, depending on preceding weather and reaction to the obstacles in its way, is in

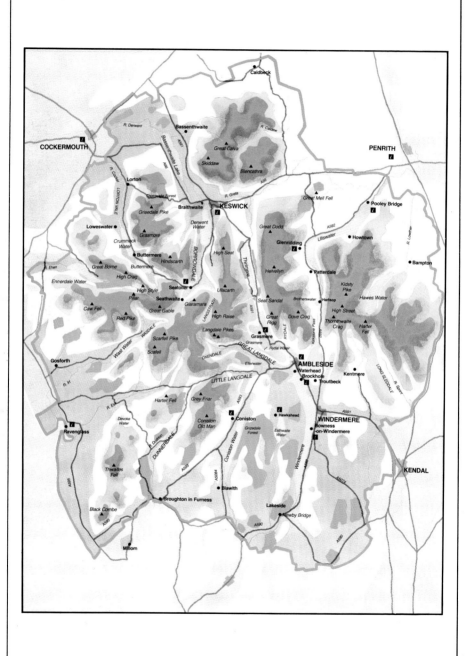

Great Gable from Wast Water.

turn angry, clamorous, boisterous or muted. Hillside colours vary with the seasons, from a score of spring-time shades of green, through yellows and golds, to rich brown, to white. And moreover, there are hourly modulations with each play of light and shade and moving cloud patterns. Rocks and crags transform as shadows lengthen. The shining levels of the waters respond to each stroke of the wind.

No other area of Britain has inspired so many writers and artists. Indeed it would be understandable if many of the uninitiated are repelled by the sheer volume of the eulogies; the struggle of poets and authors to give expression to the stirrings of often deep feelings that the beautiful area inspires. No countryside could be that idyllic! A large library could be filled with Lakeland literature – good, awful, and indifferent, old and new; but some of it the cream of the best poetry and prose in the English language.

A casual observer may well like what he sees. He could well be transfixed with admiration for it. He might even be moved to paint it, or write poetically about it. But most 'lakers' would not attempt to explain their addiction. Why does the area compel so many to travel so regularly and so far, come rain

Facing The Lake District National Park.

Bowness Bay. A tourist 'honeypot'.

or shine, to enjoy only a few hours on the hills? Why is there no shortage of volunteers to do hard, sometimes unpleasant, conservation tasks? It is surely because they love most that which they have experienced with the sweat of their brows.

To some extent the great popularity of the national park can breed an indifference, and this is fed by exaggerated reports of overcrowding. The media's iconoclasts can point to the busy promenade at Bowness, or the streets of Keswick, Ambleside or Grasmere, or the cavalcade on Striding Edge at the height of the season, and suggest that here are the examples of people destroying that which they have come to enjoy. But these are the tourist honeypots, and the busy bees among the tourists are happily gregarious. Anyone who wants peace and solitude can find it away from the main routes – even on a Bank Holiday. For outside the centres is the true Lake District. No one can live long enough to know it well. Its topography is so complex that hill walkers of many year's experience can still find unexplored corners.

The whole of Cumbria's Lakeland core lies in Britain's largest national park. Its beauty is specially protected. The freedom of the open fell country, a

privilege enjoyed here for centuries, is preserved;
and the network of public rights of way is
maintained. For the active there is the prospect of
adventure and challenge in the many forms offered
by the fells, crags, and water; for the more leisurely
inclined the easy hill and water-side walks, the
superb viewpoints, the excitement of discovery.

It was in the eighteenth century that the discovery

Walkers in Langdale.

of the Lake District really began, when the romantic
appreciation of landscape had become fashionable.
Then the artists and the first tourists flocked in, but
this must be told in another chapter. Thomas Gray
made his tour in 1769 and his account of it was
widely read. Father West, a local priest, wrote the
first guidebook in 1778: 'Such as wish to unbend the
mind from anxious care or fatiguing studies will
meet with agreeable relaxation in making the tour of
the Lakes ...' The minds of many people of quality
were unbent in the tours which followed.

The return of Cumberland-born William and
Dorothy Wordsworth to rent a cottage at Grasmere
in 1799, followed by Coleridge and Southey to
Keswick, was to set the seal of impeccable approval.
Fashionable country houses were being built by
local and immigrant gentlemen. Wordsworth
produced the first edition of his guide in 1810. In the
concluding paragraphs he expressed the hope that
the landowners would 'preserve the native beauty'
and there followed the oft-quoted lines
'... in this wish the author will be joined by persons
of pure taste throughout the whole island, who, by
their visits (often repeated) to the Lakes in the North

The Keswick boat
landings, Derwent Water.

of England, testify that they deem the district a sort of national property, in which every man has a right and interest who has an eye to perceive and a heart to enjoy'.

Britain was not without influential people of taste, and so the idea that fine landscape needed protection was born. One practical champion, a giant among men, was Canon Hardwicke Rawnsley (1851–1920), incumbent of Crosthwaite at Keswick, scholar, athlete, historian, almost a poet, traveller, impassioned lecturer and preacher, and author. He was a keen walker and compaigned for the preservation of public footpaths.

Rawnsley's first big battle was against Manchester Corporation and their proposal to dam Thirlmere for a water supply. He formed the Thirlmere Defence Association in 1877. His campaign got much sympathy, but the fight was lost in spite of the support of such giants as John Ruskin and Thomas Carlyle and Thirlmere's waters were eventually raised to drown an extra 463 acres. The threat of railway lines in the dales next occupied attention. A Buttermere Railway Bill was thrown out. An Ennerdale Railway Bill (1884) and an Ambleside Railway Bill were vigorously opposed, though the

A cartoon in *Punch* magazine, July 1883, showing the Knight of Common Sense (House of Commons Committee) rescuing the damsels of Ennerdale, Borrowdale and Derwent Water from the bad knight (the Railway Bill) who 'would have done them a fatal injury'.

bills were lost on their financial demerits. The debates were warm. Ruskin, the arbiter of good taste, objected to the engineers 'making a steam merry-go-round of the lake country'. Wordsworth wrote a sonnet and letters to the press. The former begins with the lines 'Is then no nook of English ground secure/ From rash assault?'. The argument used by James Bryce in Parliament took an interesting form, describing the Lake District as a great 'picnic-ing ground' which 'the people – look on as their national park'.

Rawnsley shared Wordsworth's concern about the danger of landowners spoiling the landscape and considered that the best way to protect the vulnerable parts of the countryside was to purchase them. With two like-minded companions: Robert Hunter, Solicitor to the Post Office, and Octavia Hill the social reformer, he founded the National Trust for Places of Historic Interest or Natural Beauty, which was registered under the Companies Act in 1895. It was (and remains so to this day) a charity, relying on gifts and public subscriptions, with the object of acquiring property to protect it for the public benefit. One of the first properties bought, in

1902, was Brandelhow Woods by the shore of Derwent Water.

Throughout the between-the-wars campaign for national parks and access to mountains, the Lake District was much on people's minds. There was a need here for firm planning policy. Access to the hills was less of a problem as walkers were free to wander on the open fell land, by let if not by right. The Lake District became a national park in 1951. The boundaries around its 880 square miles generally follow the tortuous medieval lines of the parish boundaries: roughly wavering from the A6 and the Lyth Valley in the east, to the west coast at Silecroft; in the southern line excluding Cartmel and the Furness peninsulas; and in the north omitting Penrith and taking a sweep west and north to Caldbeck then west, south west and south, omitting Cockermouth. Originally the boundary included parts of Lancashire, Westmorland and Cumberland, but in 1974 the new county of Cumbria swallowed 'Lancashire north of the Sands', the whole of Westmorland and Cumberland and nibbled at Yorkshire. The national park is therefore within one county and has a Special Planning Board with planning control within the park. Allerdale, Eden, Copeland and South Lakeland are the units providing district council service. Responsibility for the care of the the rights of way in the national park have been ceded by the county to the National Park Authority.

National park authorities do not own the land within their boundaries. However the authority *has* acquired land, including the Caldbeck Commons and Bassenthwaite Lake, the Blawith and Torver Commons, Glenridding Common (which includes the east side of Helvellyn between Striding Edge and Swirral Edge), and several broad-leaved woodlands; also scattered portions of access land, viewpoints and picnic areas to a total of 21,400 acres in 1986. The land came by gift or was an opportunity purchase.

In matters of land acquisition, the National Park Authority is not in competition with the National Trust. The Trust has come a long way since its first purchase in 1902, spurred on by generous gifts from Beatrix Potter, GM Trevelyan the historian, Sir Samuel Scott and others. It is now (in 1986) the largest landowner in the national park with 125,556 acres and a further 11,904 acres covenanted. Most of the land owned by the Trust is open to the public, but not all, for it holds eighty-six farms, effectively

Cottages at Hartsop.

A woodland walk on Windermere's shore, at Brockhole, the National Park Visitor Centre.

shielding them and the Herdwick sheep breed from the vicissitudes of modern agricultural economics. There are also seventy-seven listed buildings among the 600 which it owns in the park.

The North West Water Authority is the next largest landowner with some 38,449 acres in the Thirlmere and Haweswater catchment area. Most of the notices with dire warnings about trespass have gone. There are now footpaths by the once forbidden Thirlmere shore, and you may even sail on the precious water (but if you fall overboard swimming is not allowed!).

Thirdly, there is the Forestry Commission, with a holding of 31,453 acres to which there is free public access. At the time of writing there is a concern as to what may happen to public access if the government's plans to privatize water authorities and the Forestry Commission are ever implemented.

Access to unspoilt country is one of the main purposes of national parks and the Lake District has more of such countryside than any other. Having reached a chosen fell above the enclosed land, by one or more of the 1,500 miles of public rights of way, the fell walker has several hundred square

miles of open and varied country to freely enjoy.
For the climber there are numerous crags of great
quality. There are lakes to sail on. For the student of
nature there is great variety. There is always the
opportunity and the excitement of discovery
everywhere for those who wish 'to unbend the mind
from anxious cares'.

Brothers Water.

1 The making of the landscape

'Mountains are the beginning and the end of all natural scenery'. So said Ruskin. He spent the last twenty-nine years of his life (to 1900) looking across Coniston Water at the eastern face of Coniston Old Man.

A mountain is more than a feature in the landscape. It is petrified history, reaching back beyond the human concept of time, thrust out from the unimaginable depths, clawed and carved by the forces of the elements; standing in cold hard inanimate silence and wrinkled with the experience of millions of years. The story has a beginning. The end is only apparent, for the earth moves beneath our feet, the mountains crumble into the valleys, but in a time-scale that is almost beyond comprehension and needing a considerable mental adjustment. A reading of the history written in the Lake District landscape is mind-stretching; pursued with enthusiasm it can also be leg-stretching. But there is no need to travel far. Wordsworth compared the

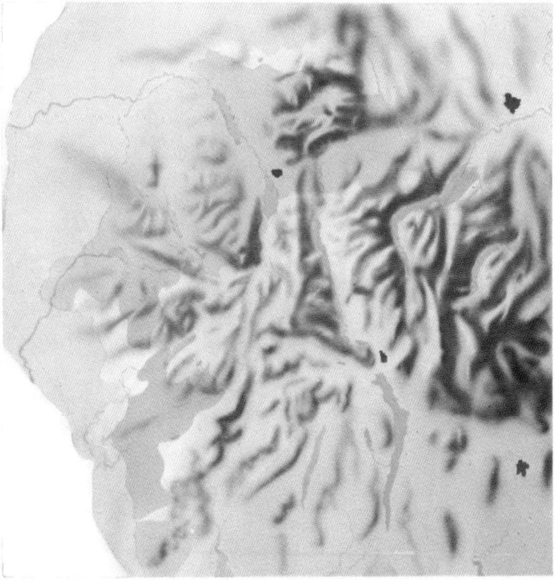

Sandstone, shale
and limestone

Granite

Skiddaw
Slate

Borrowdale
Volcanic

Silurian Slate

Simplified geological
map of the Lake District.

scenery of the Alps with that of the Lake District: the former suggesting chaos, the latter a harmony. It is a matter of scale. The Lake District's complicated geology is compressed into a uniquely small area.

An observant student of Lake District landscape could identify three generally distinct types of physical scenery. In the north and north west the mountains are great 'camel humps' fairly regular in outline. In a wide central band they are rough and craggy; and in the south mountains give way to hills, some with areas of extensive woodland. There are other less noticeable features, but more of that later. Our story begins in the north with the oldest rocks, the Skiddaw Slates, and the formative action is in the Ordovician period, 500 million years ago.

At the onset of the period with which we are concerned 'Britain' was submerged in a shallow sea. Mud and fine grit were deposited on the sea bed and over a process of many millions of years the accumulated deposits were subject to heavy pressure and hardened into rock several thousands of feet thick. This formed our Skiddaw Slate Series of rocks. One normally thinks of slate as rock which cleaves easily into plates to make roofing material. In the Skiddaw Slate the plane of cleavage is interrupted by 'minute joints' or fractures. By

weathering action, therefore, this material breaks into small fragments. Because of this there are few sharp crags in the Skiddaw Slates. Hence the rather regular unbroken outline of the mountains which it subsequently formed and which we now see, like the great hulk of Skiddaw itself (3,053 ft/931 m) brooding over Keswick, and its hefty neighbour Blencathra. The friable rock forms a soil which can

Blencathra, a Skiddaw Slate landscape, from Castlerigg stone circle.

View from Catbells looking across Skiddaw Slate country to Bassenthwaite Lake.

support woodland and moorland vegetation. The forests of Thornthwaite, about and above Bassenthwaite Lake, are on this rock. Dodd Wood, on the south-east side of the lake, where the Forestry Commission's bulldozers have cut through the rock to make tracks, is a pleasant place to examine some forms of this material. (Car park at NY 235282).

The Skiddaw Slate Series continues visibly south westwards from Skiddaw across Derwent Water towards Buttermere and Crummock Water and Loweswater and the lower half of Ennerdale. Northwards of Skiddaw it includes the rolling country 'back o' Skiddaw'. Elsewhere it is overlaid by later material, but it outcrops again in the south-westernmost corner of the Lake District in the whaleback mass of Black Combe (1,857 ft/868 m), a landmark for seafarers in the Celtic Sea. Other fell peaks in the series are the shapely Grisedale Pike and Causey Pike, seen so well in the western skyline from Castle Head, the eminence just south east of Keswick (NY 270227) which is the perfect viewpoint to observe the Skiddaw Slate Fells and to contrast them with those of the next rock sequence – the Borrowdale Volcanics.

Castle Head is thought to be a volanic 'plug' overlying a vent which is the clue to the next episode in the geological history. Towards the end of the deposition of the material in the shallow sea to form the Skiddaw Slates there were widespread earth movements. The sea bed was torn open by volcanic eruptions. Violent explosions threw out hot material from the depths of the Earth, piling it into

Climbers on Shepherd's Crag. This is Borrowdale Volcanic country, with Skiddaw Slate country beyond Derwent Water.

consolidated masses. The coarser accumulations were cemented into 'conglomerates'. There were also great outpourings of lava of varied consistences. Ashes and dust settled in great drifts. All was subject to the great pressures of subsequent earth movement, the resulting mass being about two miles thick. The Borrowdale Volcanic Series includes a huge variety of dense and heavy rock

A dramatic Borrowdale Volcanic landscape at the head of Wast Water. Great Gable is to the centre, with the slopes of Lingmell and the Scafells on the right.

Blea Tarn and the
Langdale Pikes in the
Borrowdale Volcanics.

types of great interest to students of geology. What
can be seen now in the magnificent fellscape at the
head of Borrowdale is the result of millions of years
of erosion and ice action on the bold differential
'jointings' or fracture lines of the hard rock on the
raised mountains: the rough profiles, the frowning
crags, and the deep chasms. The whole area of the
Borrowdale Volcanics from Wast Water to the
Borrowdale Fells, and eastwards across the central
area to the High Street range is a tumbled
complicated mass of peaks and cliffs and hollows
and crooked valleys; a feast for the energetic
explorer. Among others it includes the peaks of
Scafell Pike (3,210 ft/978 m), the highest point in
England; Scafell (3,162 ft/964 m) and Great Gable
(2,949 ft/899 m) with some of the finest rock climbs in
Britain; Bowfell (2,960 ft/902 m), the Langdale Pikes,
Coniston Old Man range, the Helvellyn range
(3,118 ft/950 m), Fairfield and High Street.

Some of the rocks are so hard that a vein of 'tuff' (a
consolidated fine dust), discovered by Neolithic
settlers on the high fells, was found to break
'conchoidally' like flint, and was used by them to
make stone axes. These axes have been found in
many parts of Britain and examples can be seen in

Tarn Hows at the junction of rock types: Coniston Limestone is in the foreground, with Borrowdale Volcanics in the distance.

various museums countrywide. Another type of hard rock, formed from consolidated dust and grit laid down in water, splitting into slates and taking a high polish, is quarried extensively and exported all over the world. A good place to examine this slate is in the spoil heaps of abandoned quarrying by Loughrigg Terrace (NY 346058).

At the end of the Ordovician period the high central area had not assumed the mountain shapes of today, but existed roughly in the form of a huge dome.

At this time, about 440 million years ago, there was a quieter period and much of the area was again covered by a shallow sea. Then further earth movements forced the central dome upwards and folds and fracture lines developed. Storm waters eroded the steep sides of the land dropping silt on the sea bed, with the shells of very primitive sea animals contributing to the debris. The deposits were later consolidated into what has been called the Coniston Limestone. Little of it is now visible as so much was eroded later or else overlaid. It makes no extensive contribution to the landscape, but the tracing of the narrow band exposed along the southern boundary of the Borrowdale Volcanics

The 'softer' landscape of the Silurian. Windermere from above Bowness.

from the Duddon Estuary, through the side of Coniston Old Man, through the famous beauty spot of Tarn Hows, under the head of Windermere through to Longsleddale is an exercise in observation. The rock is dark grey and can be identified by the deep wrinkles of weathering. It can be seen by the cairned viewpoint on the south east of the tarn at Tarn Hows (SD 331997). There are abandoned lime kilns on the long band, and the botanist will identify the emerald hue of grazings and the lime-favouring plants which are absent on the surrounding acidic soils.

Moving forward to a time 400 million years ago, Britain, apart from the north of Scotland, was yet again covered by the sea. Storms battered the land masses and there was massive erosion, the resulting silts settling into the deep troughs. The muds and grits which settled on the Lake District were to be acidic. The sea depths fluctuated, varying the population of sea animals. It is not known how deep the deposits were in the Lake District as much of the rock that formed was subsequently worn away; but today the remaining cover is up to two and a half miles thick. The resulting 'Silurian Slates' are generally soft and yielded easily to erosion. We see the slates now in a wide area to the south and south east. By its nature it breaks down into a soil which readily supports woodland cover and the hills are generally rounded. So we have the comparatively lush and gentle area round both shores of Windermere, by lovely Esthwaite Water, through Grizedale Forest to Coniston Water; the wooded hills and valleys east of Broughton, the Crake, the forests and woodlands of the Furness Fells; and the Winster Valley: not at all alpine but here a more passive beauty.

The Silurian Slates vary considerably according to their sequence of deposition. Geologists have listed six identifiable layers with the oldest on the northern rim and the latest in the south. A keen observer can note the differences in the many drystone walls in the area; for their builders used the material immediately to hand.

Between 350 and 400 million years ago came the violent Devonian period. There were further earth movements and the whole land mass was crushed and buckled into folds, generally running west-south-west to east-north-east. The area of the Lake District was thrust upwards out of the sea into a much higher dome. Under the enormous pressure the various rock types reacted according to their nature. The upper Silurian Slates split and shattered easily on their bedding planes, scree falling from the higher ground. The hard Borrowdale Volcanics in the centre cracked and broke into a complex pattern of troughs and arches. The effect on the easily yielding Skiddaw Slates in the north was more dramatic. The folding was severe and the zone was raised to a great height.

The earth movements opened subterranean cavities into which magma – a molten mineral 'soup' from below the earth – welled upwards, forcing its way on through faults and fissures. The enormous heat changed the rock with which it made contact, physically and chemically. Condensing vapours crystalized into minerals which were later to be exploited by man. The magma, cooling more slowly under the lean earth surface, formed the subsequently exposed Cumbrian Granites. The most famous area is at Shap, where the hard dome of rock has been extensively quarried. Shap Granite provided building blocks for some of London's famous buildings – St Pancras Station and the Albert Memorial, for example. There are other granite intrusions observable which are assumed to date from this period. A granite, pigmented with iron, is

The Ravenglass and Eskdale narrow-gauge railway. Now a tourist attraction, once used to transport iron ore and granite from Eskdale's mines and quarries.

In upper Eskdale.

exposed in a wide area from Eskdale, through Miterdale to Wasdale. The pink blocks can be seen in many of the drystone walls. There were quarries in Eskdale and the present narrow-gauge railway to Ravenglass, much loved by holidaymakers, once transported the blocks. Other smaller areas of granitic intrusions occur in the Skiddaw Slates, and the minerals about them have been mined, notably on the Carrock and Caldbeck Fells.

In the fifty million years of the Devonian period arid conditions prevailed and sandstorms rasped away the upper surfaces of the rocks. At times there were periods of prolonged storms and floods which also wore away the surface and exploited the channels formed by the faults. Vast quantities of materials were dispersed into the seas to the south.

The level of this southern sea rose and spread northwards, but was shallow over the Lake District's dome. By this time (270 to 350 million years ago) there were more advanced life forms. In the sea were corals, brachiapods, molluscs and colonies of crinoids ('sea lilies' – animals attaching themselves to the sea bed by a jointed stem). The remains of these animals accumulated into thick beds in the shallow sea and were compacted to form the white

Carboniferous Limestone. This was later eroded from the central area of the Lake District but can be seen today around the southern and north-eastern fringes of the park. At its edge it forms ramparts or ridges best seen at Whitbarrow Scar, most of which is a nature reserve and Site of Special Scientific Interest; and Scout Scar west of Kendal from which (SD 487919) there are magnificent views over the Limestone areas, across the Silurian plain, to the distant volcanics of the central fells.

The level of the Carboniferous sea fluctuated. The limestones were often exposed at the surface and mud and silt were washed down from the nearby land surface and enclosed between the sheets of pure limestone. As the sea became even more shallow, silts and marine grits were laid down and marginal swamps became the sites of coal measure forests, where masses of vegetation accumulated in layers between river-borne clays and sands. Today these coal measures remain only in west Cumbria where they formed the basis for the prosperity of towns like Workington and Whitehaven. Some of this wealth found its way into the Lake District in the late eighteenth and early nineteenth century in the acquisition and improvement of estates, and the building of fine houses. The Curwen family of Workington bought the Belle Isle property on Windermere, and much of the beautiful wooded west shore (now owned by the National Trust) owes its existence to them.

By the end of the Carboniferous times the Lake District must have been buried under several thousand feet of Carboniferous sediments. Another phase of mountain building then began in north-west Europe.

In the Lake District the thrust came south of the earlier centre of uplift but the result was the elevation of the central dome, opening up old faults and cracking open new ones. It is thought that at this time the effects of vapourization of raised volcanic material produced the minerals such as the copper mined in the Coniston Old Man range and lead mined above Glenridding on Helvellyn; probably also included, though not by all geologists, were the haematite (iron) veins, the exploitation of which was to have an important effect on the area's industrial history.

At this time the equator lay somewhere around 200 to 300 miles away from our region and conditions were again arid. The exposed rocks were blasted by sandstones. The Carboniferous

Glenridding, Ullswater. A typical U-shaped glaciated valley on the east side of the Helvellyn range. The hanging valley of Keppel Cove is at the valley head. Birkhouse Moor is left, and Sheffield Pike right.

Limestone cover was stripped from the higher land. Desert sands, red because of their iron content, covered the lower land to the west, south west and the north east. This formed the rock known as 'New Red Sandstone'. This rock forms the dramatic sea cliffs favoured by sea birds at St Bees Head (regrettably outside the national park). The stone can be seen in the magnificent ruin of Furness Abbey near Barrow, and Calder Abbey (NY 051063), the quarry for which was in the national park's woodland (NY 055068).

About sixty million years ago came the great Alpine uplift of the Tertiary period, which built major mountain chains like the Alps, Rockies and Himalayas. Almost the whole of the area of the British Isles, still then connected to the Continent, was lifted out of the sea. The Lake District's central dome took the main thrust around the Scafells and the whole was raised to a greater height than it is today. The profile was not rugged at this stage, but the drainage pattern developed roughly along the river lines as we now see them. Erosion exploited the faults and cracks contained by the harder rocks but broke through the softer ones. The climate then was mild, vegetation was rich, and animals we now

associate with sub-tropical areas roamed the forests of the hills and valleys.

Then the coming of the Ice Ages brought about a calamitous change of climate in the Northern Hemisphere one and half million years ago, the cause of which has never been conclusively explained. Winter snows, never melting in the cool summers, accumulated and became consolidated in vast ice fields. At its peak the ice sheets covered Scandinavia and Russia and spread over the continent of America as far south as Illinois. Britain was covered to the north of a line between the Severn and the Thames. At the peak of accumulation in the Lake District the valleys must have been filled, and the whole area almost covered by ice, only the highest summits remaining clear. Ice striations on the rocks can be seen at a height of 2,500 ft (760 m) on the Scafells.

There were several glacial periods. It is not easy to adduce how many as each subsequent advance wiped out much of the evidence of the earlier; and there have been lesser advances. The last marked period was probably about 15,000 years ago. On each occasion the pattern of glaciation would follow the outlines of its predecessor. If (perhaps one

Great Gable from the Scafells. The cloud level is at about the height of the maximum ice covering. Only the Lake District's highest peaks were uncovered.

should say 'when') another glacial period was to begin it would do so from an accumulation of snow high on the colder north- and east-facing hollows (called 'coves' or 'coombes' in the Lake District, 'corries' or 'cwms' in Scotland and Wales respectively) for even now, after hard winters, snow and ice lingers long in the coves after it has melted elsewhere on the fells.

Glacier ice formed from compacted snow is unlike water ice in that it is granular and a plastic-like mass of it flows downhill. The progress is slow but sure, as it is in the case of Alpine or Greenland glaciers today. Before the first Ice Age the Lake District was a large central dome of rock with fissures left by successive uplifts. These had become the river valleys and had been worn by the waters into a 'V' shaped cross-section. The whole was covered in vegetation and inhabited by animals. At the time of the greatest ice cap, ice flowed outward from the whole area, following the existing river valleys, descending into what is now the Celtic Sea to the west, and spilling out southwards across the Cheshire plain. The northern movement of Lakeland ice was blocked and turned by the ice descending from Scotland and so the

Deepdale in the north-east side of Fairfield. There are several coves in the hanging valley at the head.

mass turned west to plough out the Solway Firth, and east through the Tyne Gap.

In the interglacial periods the covering would not have been great and indeed, interglacial climates could be warmer than those of today. One must imagine that from the central dome the ice flowed downwards through the river valleys. The surface ice moves faster than the deeper ice, which is slowed down by friction. As the glacier advances, it drags along rock debris which acts as a 'grater' on the valley floor. Water takes the easy way, turning and twisting through the hard rock spurs of the valley-sides. A heavy glacier, though slow moving, bulldozes its way. Spurs of the valley are eroded away and become truncated. The valley becomes much deepened and 'U' shaped. The mass of ice in the main valley has much more erosive powers than the smaller glaciers in the side valleys, so the latter are left 'hanging' above very steeply plunging walls. The lower parts of the valley are receiving ice from several tributary sources. The weight of it is enormous and the movement irresistible as the mass grinds downwards, and the original river valleys are over-deepened. So the lakes are formed. A glance at a map confirms their disposition, radiating outwards from the central Lake District.

The hanging valleys provide attractive landscape features. Water from them spills down the steep walls of the main valley. After prolonged rain this provides a spectacle, well displayed for instance when looking across the Buttermere Valley to Red Pike and High Stile. Ribbons of white water drop down the crags and Sour Milk Gill looks well named. There are many waterfalls and everyone has favourites. Taylor Gill Force at the head of Borrowdale is one of the best though its approach is rough and requires one to have a head for heights. Piers Gill on the north side of Scafell Pike is another spectacle for fell walkers on the path from Wasdale to Styhead – particularly in a gale when up-draughts blow and scatter spray and spume into angry spouts and fountains. In Victorian times waterfall visits by tourists were obligatory. Itineraries would include Tilberthwaite Gill north of Coniston (NY 305009); Dungeon Ghyll in Langdale; the deservedly popular Falls of Lodore behind the Lodore Hotel in Borrowdale; Stock Ghyll in the wooded gorge at Ambleside; and of course Aira Force, Ullswater, (NY 400205) where a suitably sickening legend of

Aira Force, by Ullswater, in winter. One of the more spectacular of the many waterfalls, it is owned by the National Trust.

tragic love had been invented to add spice to the
visit.

One major glacial feature in the landscape of the
high fells is the cove. Nowadays snow lingers long
in these high north- and east-facing rock basins. It
was where each glaciation began and ended. For
long periods of the year they were not reached by
sunshine; ice and frost has eaten into the mountains

Stickle Tarn in a cove in
the Langdale Pikes. Pavey
Ark is behind.

and deepened the hollows in milder periods, as
now, leaving meltwater tarns.

These mountain tarns can be startlingly beautiful:
still waters contrasting with the rough cliffs of the
cove. Goats Water sitting under the great frowning
face of Dow Crag on Coniston Old Man is an
example easily reached by the moderate walker. To
the south west of it Blind Tarn is another good
example. Stickle Tarn in Langdale under Pavey Ark
is another, not marred by the low dam wall built to
maintain a head of water to a valley mill. Others
which can be enjoyed by fell walkers include Red
Tarn on Helvellyn, Bleaberry Tarn under Red Pike,
Buttermere, Angle Tarn under Bow Fell, Bowscale
Tarn under Bowscale Fell, Scales Tarn under
Blencathra, and Blea Water and Small Water under
High Street.

A fell can have several coves biting into the
summit. As these are widened by erosion, crest-like
ridges develop between them, some quite slender.
So on the east side of Helvellyn, we have Striding
Edge, the most exciting and popular way up the
mountain, the ridge between Nethermost Cove and
Red Tarn Cove; and on the other side of the latter,
between it and Brown Cove, is Swirral Edge.
Another good example is Sharp Edge between the

Striding Edge on Helvellyn in winter. It is a ridge between the deep bites of Red Tarn Cove and Nethermost Cove.

coves of Scales Tarn and Foule Crag Cove on Blencathra.

Other features in the glaciated landscape are the many hummocks of terminal moraines, piles of debris left at the snout of glaciers as the ice stopped, dumped its load and then retreated. Hollows within some of the moraines have been left by melting cores of stranded ice. There is a good example of a moraine field at the head of Dunmail Raise between Grasmere and Thirlmere, and at the head of Stake Pass, Langdale.

As the glaciers bit into the valley-sides, frost-shattered fragments of rock, some of them quite large, fell into the ice and were carried forward. Some of these were carried long distances: boulders of Shap Granite, for instance, have been dropped on the Pennines and as far east as the Yorkshire coast. Ice-smoothed Borrowdale Volcanic boulders have been found as far south as Cheshire. More locally these 'erratics' can be identified in surprising places: volcanic fragments sit on limestone 'pavements' or in Silurian woodlands. Some of the boulders are left oddly perched; one such is the famous path-side Bowder Stone in Borrowdale (NY 254164), one of the most photographed stones in Britain.

Scratch marks or striations on ice-smoothed bedrock can be seen in numerous places. Some

Bassenthwaite Lake. This was once one with Derwent Water but was separated by an alluvial plain.

rocks are honed smooth and sloping on the side facing the ice flow, and are steep and rougher on the other side where the ice has nibbled away morsels of rock. The effect is supposed to resemble a sleeping sheep, known to geomorphologists as a 'roche-moutonnée'; which must mean that imagination is as essential an asset to a serious academic as it is to all others who enjoy interpreting a glaciated landscape.

The advance of the ice scraped the landscape clear of soil. In the aftermath of glaciation, storms and flash floods attacked the bare tree-less landscape. At these times some of the lakes received large quantities of silt. Buttermere and Crummock were obviously once one large lake, but have been divided by alluvial deposits. Similarly Bassenthwaite Lake and Derwent Water can still be united during serious floods. Some of the present valleys probably once held lakes; Langdale might be one of them. And meanwhile, the continuing deposition of river sediments is gradually reducing the area of the lakes.

About ten thousand years ago, alpine and tundra vegetation colonized the fells, followed in turn by birch and pine, willow and alder, and then with oak forest growing to a height of 2,500 ft (760 m). Animals including elk, bears and wolves repopulated the area as the climate became milder. All was ripe for the next episode – human settlement.

2 **Early human settlement**

In 1984, under artificial lights and the eye of a TV camera, a birch tree was felled by a national park ranger in Grizedale Forest. Trees are felled there most days so why the media attention? First, it was felled with an axe, which in our mechanical age is practically unheard of; but secondly the axe was something like four thousand years old.

Stone-axe making was the Lake District's first major industry. Major it was, for the axe 'factory' sites are still being discovered as outcrops of the 'tuff' (an extremely hard rock formed from volcanic dust, from which the axes were made) are investigated. The first site was found in Langdale in 1947 and identifiable 'Langdale' stone axes are in many museums, for the industry enjoyed export trade to many parts of Britain. The axes were roughed out on site with granite hammers then

Trees in Langdale, the birth place of the Neolithic stone axe.

taken down to the coast to be sharpened and polished on sandstone. Neolithic man was not a primitive. He wore woollen clothing, cultivated crops, kept domestic animals and made pottery; and he was also a craftsman. A finished axe is a thing of beauty and precision.

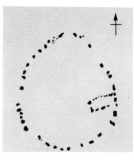

Castlerigg stone circle.

But it was the Neolithic axe and the torch that made the first great changes to the Lake District environment. Before then, in the Mesolithic period, human activity among the wooded hills and valleys was limited to hunting. The only discovered sign of settlement for that time is at Eskmeals on the coast, where the hunters also used the fish resources of the coast and river. But the use of the axe in Neolithic times made it possible to create clearances in the forest which covered the whole area, for domestic animals and cultivation. The proof of extensive clearances has been found by pollen analysis of lake sediments. Pollen is a hard, practically indestructible material, each species identifiable under the microscope. When a core of sediment is obtained from the bottom of a lake bed and taken to a laboratory (in a special process perfected by the Freshwater Biological Association at Windermere) the oldest deposits from the early formation of the lake to those of more recent times are revealed in it from base to top. Pollens can be identified in each and can be dated by radiocarbon techniques. The decline of the forest is clearly shown to have begun during the expansion of Neolithic settlement, revealed by a decrease in the amount of tree pollens then and an increase in grass pollens. In the rough, central Lake District the clearings were doubtlessly made for stock pasturage. This was the cause, and the beginning, of the soil impoverishment and erosion on the hills which continued through the centuries. On the deeper soils of the coastal plains there is evidence of crop cultivation from the very earliest times.

Relatively little is known of Neolithic man and how he lived. Of his wooden buildings there is scant sign, but the great mysteries include the significance of his stone henges and circles which in the Lake District were built in the late Neolithic and early Bronze Ages. A ritualistic use is assumed, but they might also have been tribal meeting places and centres for trading. One of the most picturesque and most photographed stone circles of any in Britain, because of its setting, with a wrap-around backcloth of Skiddaw, Blencathra, Helvellyn and the eastern fells of Borrowdale, is at Castlerigg (National Trust) east of Keswick (NY 291236). In former times it was called the 'Druids' Circle' but of course it was there for millennia before the arrival of Iron Age culture. It is a moody place changing with light and cloud shadow. The poet Keats saw it on a wet day:

> . . . a dismal cirque
> Of Druid stones, upon a forlorn moor,
> When the chill rain begins at shut of eve,
> In dull November, and their chancel vault,
> Th' Heaven itself, is blinded throughout night.'

The 'circle' is in fact slightly oval, some 100 feet by 109 feet (30.5 m by 33 m). An oblong internal setting of a further ten stones is still a puzzle.

Another circle, slightly smaller and more symmetrical with a closer cluster of fifty stones, is at Swinside, tucked away under an eastern spur of Black Combe (SD 171882). It is on private land but easily viewable from the nearby footpath. There are a few other smaller stone circles apart from those more properly identified as small stone rings or 'kerbs' built around ancient tombs. One attractive little circle is in a moorland area rich in ancient

Swinside stone circle.

burial sites. Called locally 'The cockpit', it is on Askham Fell (NY 483223). To the north east of this is Mayburgh henge. It is too near to the M6 (NY 519284) to have any strong religious atmosphere now and it is in the care of English Heritage. It is of the late Neolithic/early Bronze Age, built of several thousand tons of round 'beck-bottom' stones encircling an enclosure about 330 ft (100 m) across. There were originally some standing stones within the circle, but apart from one, they were removed in the eighteenth century. Just across the road to the south east is the oddly named 'King Arthur's Round Table', a ditch and bank construction of the henge type of a slightly later date. The placing of henges at ancient cross-roads must have some significance. Eight miles to the south at Shap at one time was a circle and an avenue of stones, for Camden, the Elizabethan historian, recorded it. This must have been an important site but it has been broken up and destroyed. Traces can be found by the archaeologist's practised eye. There remains the re-erected and impressive 'Goggleby Stone' west of the village.

It can be assumed that the Bronze Age culture penetrated the relatively isolated Lake District later

Castlerigg stone circle, near Keswick, dating from late Neolithic times or early Bronze Age.

than most areas. Stone axes would still be used efficiently after bronze smithing was introduced. The bronze implements found were most probably 'imports'. The major settlements of the period have been recognized outside the national park to the south and east. However, in the Early and Middle Bronze Age the climate was milder making possible cultivation of some of the district's upland areas as is evidenced in the west by the cairn fields on Burnmoor, Birker Fell, and Ennerdale Forest, and in the east on Moor Divock and Shap. The visible remains of ancient settlements are difficult to date, particularly as sites very often have settlements of later periods superimposed on the earlier. One group of settlement enclosure-remains at Aughertree Fell, four miles west of the village of Caldbeck, is encircled by banks and ditches with platforms for buildings, probably circular, within. The banks were probably bases for wooden stockades. There is no evidence of internal buildings in the central enclosure which has a sunken lane leading to it. A Bronze Age burial mound nearby yielded twelve urns when it was dug into during last century.

Burial cairns in very many places have been destroyed by the amateur archaeologists of the nineteenth century. The scatterings of other stone heaps often originated from field clearances prior to cultivation.

It is assumed that the hill settlements were evacuated following a change to a cooler, wetter climate towards the end of the Bronze Age. Farming in the Lake District from that time on became more difficult, the land only fit for summer grazing.

3 **The Roman occupation**

If you leave the road at the top of Hardknott Pass and walk a short way westwards under the crags of Border End you are confronted with a sight which must stir the imagination; for on a shelf, a mere step on the tumbled mass of rock and fell over 400 feet below, are perched the remarkable ruins of a Roman fort. You are looking back over 1,800 years of human history. To get to this place the Romans had first to engineer their road, sometimes through solid rock, over the passes of Wrynose and Hardknott, and one can only marvel at their amazing tenacity, for if the uncompromising topography was not enough, every niche on the fells, every piece of woodland here at that time, could hide hostile guerillas.

A walk among the ruins is no less astonishing. The fort stands on an 800 ft (244 m) high spur and the view is tremendous. Northwards, across an abyss over the Esk you are faced with the Scafells, the highest land in England, a mass of steep green fell heaving into the distance, broken by rock barriers, crags and clefts. Walking westwards you can see clear down the delectably lush Esk Valley, patterned with walls, trees and farmsteads, across ten miles to the sea beyond. And most of the builders of this airy outpost had marched all the way from Dalmatia – modern-day Yugoslavia.

Before the Romans arrived the territory of the turbulent Brigantes tribe stretched over the whole of the North of England; a sub-group known as the Carvettii occupied the Lake District. In an area where geographical conditions favour a scattering of small settlements the tribe would really be a very loose confederation of clans. Indeed the Romans record that the weakness of the Britons generally was their lack of cohesion into organized fighting units. Fight they certainly could, for they prided themselves on their prowess in arms, but their first loyalty was probably to their own small clan. The clan system was to dominate the Border country for many centuries in spite of the coming of new cultures and civilizations.

It is likely that in the Lake District the tribal settlements were small, but the land offered a lot of

Hardknott Roman fort, the north-west gate leading to the precipice, and looking to the highest land in England, the Scafells.

scope for guerilla warfare. It has been suggested that one Brigantian stronghold was on the summit plateau of Carrock Fell north of Blencathra, for here is the ruin of a large hillfort over 800 ft by 400 ft (244 m by 122 m), built of hundreds of tons of stone. There is evidence that part of the wall was deliberately pulled down by the Romans. Hillforts are difficult to date without costly excavations and some may have been re-occupied or constructed after Roman times. Remains of a spectacular stone-walled stronghold can be seen on Castle Crag, south of Grange in Borrowdale. Traces of another are on Castle Crag on the fell north west of Thirlmere. There is another at Castle Howe, on a wooded hill by the old road side near the Pheasant Hotel, north west of Bassenthwaite Lake.

The Romans probably first reached the eastern side of the district from their base at York after they had won a decisive victory over the Brigantes in AD 74. But trouble in the south and in Wales prevented further action until AD 79 when Gnaeus Julius Agricola brought his armies north from Chester. The Roman system of conquest was to build roads, defended at intervals by forts, first of turf and wood and only later by stone. The troops were required not only to be an efficient disciplined fighting force, but also pick-and-shovel engineers. The north-bound road reached Watercrook south east of Kendal, where a fort was built, then went north eastwards and north via the cross-roads at Brougham, to Penrith and Carlisle, which was to become the important administrative centre of the area. Having presumably pacified the clans in the Eden Valley to the east of the Lake District and those on the Solway Plain, attention would then be given to containing those in the Lake District valleys. A road was driven north-west from Watercrook to Waterhead, Ambleside, where a fort (Galava) was built at the head of Windermere. From here a road ran eastwards, probably via Troutbeck, then one route ran along the magnificent ridgeway 2,000 feet up on High Street. Traces of this road, along what is

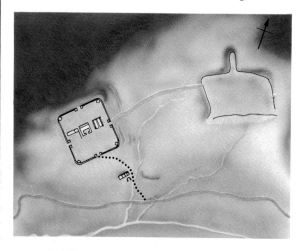

Plan of Hardknott Roman fort and parade ground.

now a bridleway on the high fell, can still be seen. The road must have finished at the fort at Brougham. Why take the high ridge? It was probably an 'improvement' job on an existing British road following an obvious line *above* the swamps and becks of the lower land, and used for patrol duties.

Another more important road ran westwards; but first of Galava itself. The stones have long since been 'quarried' for local building, but in Borrans field ('Borrans' is an old Norse name for 'heap of stones') the foundations can be seen (NY 373034). The first fort was of turf and timber. Later, probably when Trajan (98–117) was strengthening the Roman hold, it was rebuilt of stone and sited slightly differently on an artificial mound, above the reach of

Hardknott Roman fort with Eskdale Valley behind.

floods. There are signs that the fort was attacked and burned, probably twice. In the museum at Kendal is a gravestone from the site which reads, when translated, 'To the Good God of the Underworld: Flavius Romanus, Record Clerk. Lived for 35 years. Killed in the fort by the enemy'.

The road westwards cuts right across the Lake District to the coast and the Roman port at Ravenglass. No long straight lines here, for from Little Langdale the engineers were faced with savage slopes in extremely rough terrain, over Wrynose and Harknott Passes. Parts of the road can still be traced.

So to Hardknott Roman fort, Mediobogdum, on its airy shelf. Not only was it well placed to observe movements in the Esk Valley, it was also in a formidable defensive position. The land falls sharply on the south west and south east. On the north west the rock is sheer over Eskdale. Only the north-east side was vulnerable and here a deep trench was dug. Much of the stone has been carted away, but even so there is plenty to see. The fort is 375 feet (114 m) square, and defended by ramparts: earth banks on the inside piled against the stout stone wall; and at each corner there was a tower, the bases of which can be seen. Roman forts had gates in the middle of each wall and Hardknott is no exception, even though the one on the north west leads on to a cliff; a possible nasty hazard for a sentry on a dark night. The main gate, over twenty-two feet wide, faces the modern road, and the interior follows the regulation pattern with roads ruled straight across from gate to gate, the one from side to side being the *Via Principalis*, the one from the main gate being the *Via Praetoria* which leads to the headquarters building. The entrance to this is through a courtyard, partly enclosed by two 'L' shaped cloisters, part of which may have been enclosed to form rooms. Beyond is the hall or basilica, where the officers would report to the commandant. Behind this are three rooms, the centre one being the regimental chapel.

On the right of the headquarters is the granary, 54 ft by 22 ft (16 m by 6.5 m); so important that it had to be the strongest building in the fort: damp-, vermin-, and attack-proof. This would have comfortably held a substantial grain store for the garrison of 500 men. On the other side of the headquarters building is the commandant's house. The troops lived in wooden buildings, probably six of them, in the front half of the fort.

Below the fort towards the road is the bath-house. It has from east to west, a cold plunge bath, a cold room, a warm room, and a hot room, with the furnace beyond supplying under-floor heating. Below is the round *laconicum*, a hot-dry 'sweating' room which probably had a domed roof. Outside, 250 yards from the fort, on the north-east side is a most remarkable feature. A parade ground covering about three acres of land has been levelled into the hillside by cutting out on the north side and using the material to form an embankment to the south. This on terrain, anything but horizontal,

The Esk estuary at Ravenglass.

and littered by heavy rocks! There is an artificial mound, the saluting base, where the commanding officer would stand.

The gate inscription suggests that the fort dates from the reign of Emperor Hadrian (117–38). Its occupation by auxiliary troops may not have been continuous but it was probably abandoned before the end of the second century when it would have been left with caretakers as a staging post until the end of the fourth century.

From Hardknott the road, traceable in places, went down Eskdale to the Roman port, village and fort of Glannaventa at Ravenglass. Hardknott is not visible from here, but one beacon on Muncaster Fell would have served for communication. Ravenglass, at the confluence of the Esk and the Mite, was probably a British port before the occupation. Little can be seen of the Roman fort, for it has been completely robbed of stone and damaged by the railway line and the sea. But to the east of the fort in woodland one remarkable part of it remains: the bath-house, long called 'Walls Castle' (SD 088961). With its walls remaining at the original height of twelve feet it is the most upstanding Roman building remaining in the north of England, but its vulnerability to curious visitors must be cause for concern.

From Ravenglass a road probably went northwards for it was necessary to link up with the coastal defence system right round the west coast and the Solway to Hadrian's Wall. The wall was begun in 122 following Emperor Hadrian's visit to Britain, and marked the northern frontier of the Roman Empire. But it had other purposes too: firstly the obvious one of holding back the Scottish tribes; but secondly it undoubtedly served to prevent the potentially deadly alliance of those tribes with the Brigante clans in the occupied territory, who may have profited from trade with the Romans, but as experience proved, were liable to take advantage of any sign of weakness. The wall also controlled movement to and from the Empire.

The Roman occupation was hardly an instant in history for it lasted over 300 years and had a great influence culturally and administratively long after the Romans had left. The Roman fighting units were withdrawn very early in the fifth century when Emperor Honorius ordered the British to look after themselves, as best they could.

4 **The Dark Ages**

The departure of Roman order left some chaos. There is little archaeological or documentary evidence to suggest what happened next in the Lake District; it is mainly legend and folklore. The Dark Ages had their glimmer of light. There is evidence that the Romans and Romano-British at Hadrian's Wall had come to know the Christian faith before the fourth century. There is a theory that St Patrick was a Romano-British Cumbrian, taken to Ireland by pirates as a slave, and that he eventually returned to his native countryside as a missionary. Patterdale (earlier 'Patrikdale') has its church and its old well dedicated to him. It has been suggested that another missionary, St Kentigern, (later Bishop of Glasgow) preached in the area, for a number of churches in the north of Cumbria are dedicated to him. Caldbeck church in the national park is one of these as is the church at the village of Mungrisdale, under Skiddaw, which takes its name from the saint's other, Celtic, nomenclature, St Mungo, 'the loved one'. It is however probable that the dedications are evidence of a cult in the tenth century, when northern Cumbria was in the Kingdom of Strathclyde. One resident was St Herbert, close friend of St Cuthbert of Lindisfarne. It was supposed that the saint set up a cell on Derwent Water's largest island, St Herbert's Isle, which became a place of pilgrimage.

From the seventh century Anglian natives and settlers increased their influence. East of the Pennines was their kingdom of Northumbria. A western movement throughout England confined British territory to the moors of the South West, the hills of Wales, and north-west England and Scotland. The British of Wales and the north west called themselves 'The Cymry' (hence later 'Cumberland' and 'Cumbria'; the *Anglo-Saxon Chronicle* called the north-west corner of England and Strathclyde 'Cumbraland'). The area was part of the Scottish kingdom of Strathclyde whose southern boundary was somewhat mobile, and remained so over some subsequent centuries. Some of the old British language survives in place-names. Helvellyn has

The ninth-century Anglian cross at Irton.

that ring about it. 'Pen' for hill or head appears in Penrith and Penruddock. 'Blaen' (a summit) occurs in Blencathra. Many river names are British. One, perhaps dubious, question has been posed: were the native British employed by the later settlers as shepherds? It is suggested that this would explain why a farmer from a local family can today, for amusement, recite the old 'Celtic' method of counting his sheep. There are several versions which might have a slightly familiar ring to a Welsh speaker. The north Lakes version of one to ten is 'yan, tyan, tethera, methera, pimp, sethera, lethera, hovera, dovera, dick'. 'Yan' for one, and 'yance' for once is still commonly used in the rich local dialect.

As the English speakers came westwards into Cumbria it is most probable that they occupied the more fertile lower land. They were Christians. There is remarkable evidence of this at Irton churchyard where stands, ten feet high, a well preserved ninth century Anglian cross. It is covered in decoration: vine scrolls, steps, frets, and rosettes. If a front panel did once have runes they have been weathered completely away.

Most fragments of Anglian sculptured stones have been found outside the central Lake District.

However, fragments have been found at Dacre, north of Ullswater. Bede referred to a Dacre Monastery. The Norman church is now on this site, but very recent archaeological digs around the church have revealed some traces there of what is almost certainly evidence of a monastic establishment. This includes part of the cemetery, a timber building, a monastic drain, and some Anglo-Saxon artifacts.

In the churchyard at Gosforth by the national park's western boundary stands a beautifully long slender sandstone cross – some thirteen feet high. It looks strangely incongruous among the modern tombstones. Closer examination must raise the pulse rate of any historian. Firstly it is over a thousand years old, and secondly without any doubt it was carved in the Viking tradition. The Vikings came first as raiders, but in the final settlement many came as Christians. Christian yes, but the sculptor of this cross seemed to have kept his options open; for on one side of it is the Christian story of the triumph of good over evil, while on the other sides the same tale is told according to Viking mythology. The base of the cross is a stylistic representation of the bark of an ash tree; for it is

One of four stone bears of unknown origin in Dacre churchyard, the site of an ancient monastery.

Detail on the Viking cross at Gosforth. Loki, the evil one, is lying, bound, in the pit.

The Gosforth Viking cross.

Yggdrasill the sacred ash tree, giver of life. On the east side Christ is crucified and a soldier is piercing his side with his sword. On the other sides Odin and the other gods face the powers of evil. Loki, the evil one, is bound hand and foot and cast into a pit for his crafty slaying of the god Balder. Heimdal, the sleepless one who can see for a hundred miles and can hear the grass grow, guards with his horn Bifrost the flaming rainbow bridge to Asgard the realm of the gods; and the god Vidar fights off the evil Ferris Wolf, here shown as a two-headed dragon. Part of the Norse tradition of Ragnarok – Doomsday – is also illustrated.

By the eighth century Vikings had occupied the Orkneys and Shetlands, the islands and the west coast of Scotland, Ireland, and the Isle of Man, where they intermarried with Celts. From their bases they no doubt raided the coasts of north-west England from time to time. Their move into the Lake District may have been precipitated by the action of the Norse king Harald Finehair. The theory is based on an account by the thirteenth-century Icelandic historian Snorri Sturluson, though one must be cautiously aware that he blamed Harald Finehair for a great deal. Sturluson states that when Harald Finehair gained power over Norway (*c.* 900) he made an arrangement whereby each of his many 'fylkes' (territories) was governed by an earl. Inevitably there were disputes when rule was so remote. It seems that his authority was challenged in the area of Orkney, Shetland, west Scotland and the Isle of Man. Warships were sent to settle accounts and they did a useful job until they reached Man, where they found the island deserted of inhabitants and their goods. They had 'fled all folk into Scotland'. Why Scotland when the Cumbrian coast was the nearest land-fall? But Cumbria at that time *was* part of Scotland. They must have found their new land very acceptable as then the central Lake District was unfarmed.

Many of the Viking settlers were Christians. The extent of their settlement is seen tangibly in the number of Norse/Celtic wheel-head crosses, and hog-back tombs in the churches and churchyards scattered throughout Cumbria. Inside the church at Gosforth are two typically Scandinavian 'hog-back' tombstones, one carved with a battle scene. Other stone fragments there include the 'fishing stone', which depicts two men fishing from a boat with an abundance of fish. A cross fragment has Thor fishing for the World Serpent and a hart trampling on

snakes. In all, 115 Viking-age carvings have been found across thirty-six sites in Cumbria, most of these in the south and west, and there are similarities in style to stones found in south-west Scotland. Some stones have been built into church walls during restoration periods.

Applethwaite, under Skiddaw. One of the many 'thwaites'.

There is much evidence also of Viking in the place-names: the dales (dalr), the fells (fjall), streams are 'becks' (bekkr), the tarns (tjorn), waterfalls are 'forces' (foss). The suffix in place-names of 'thwaite', Norse/Irish for clearing or meadow, is common: Rosthwaite, Satterthwaite, Braithwaite, Seathwaite. Similarly the word 'saetr', a shieling or summer pasture: Hawkshead, Seat Sandal, Seatoller, Ambleside (Amal's shieling), Seatallan. Place-names sometimes refer to the use of areas: Swindale is the dale of the swine; Grisedale, or Grizedale (there are sixteen of these in the Lake District) is the dale of the pigs. There are numerous other examples of place-names with Norse words. For instance 'blea' for blue and 'how' for hill are extremely common.

Norse words also occur in the dialect. 'Brant' for steep (eg Brantwood, Ruskin's house); 'seaves' are rushes (sef); 'slape' for slippery; 'laikin' for playing is well known. 'Stee' for ladder probably explains the place-name for Styhead. If anyone has climbed up the steep – or should one say 'brant' – track up to the high cross-roads on the fells 'ladder top' seems descriptive. Many more obscure dialect words, especially used in farming, may well have Norse origins.

There is an absence of visible settlement sites which can be definitely identified as Scandinavian. Many will have been built upon later by farms, hamlets and villages. For their locations one must rely on place-names. The practice of using 'sheilings', summer settlements in the high lands, should yield some evidence as there is less possibility of these having later buildings superimposed. There is scope for research and some is being done in a limited way. One difficulty is that the summer shelters would be crude structures. There *are* traces of old enclosures and possible hut foundations in some of the higher valleys where shielings would be established: for instance in Mickleden at the head of Langdale.

There are in existence a large number of 'bank barns' built of stone which would formerly have most probably been built of wood. These are barns built into a slope with a lower floor sitting into the hillside, and an upper one at a higher ground level allowing hay to be carted in and dropped through a hatch to the stock below. It has been suggested by historians that their concentration in the Lake District – more than anywhere else in Britain – shows the Viking agricultural influence, for bank barns are very common in Scandinavia. The idea is interesting but it might be just a sensible adaptation to the steep terrain.

5 **From medieval times**

Two and a half miles outside the national park by Eamont Bridge is a mish-mash of roads: going north and south the old A6 and its replacement the M6; east and west the A66 and the A686 linked with several 'B' roads and with attendant roundabouts. It has been a busy cross-roads since at least Roman times. Brocavum, the Roman fort which defended it with a thousand men, was just to the east at the confluence of the Rivers Lowther and Eamont. Little sign of it remains for much of the stone was used to build the magnificent red sandstone castle, dating from the late twelfth century, the substantial ruin of which remains (English Heritage NY 538290). Its enormous bulk is testimony to the effective feudal order introduced by the Normans.

The wild country of the Lake District was of little interest to the Normans at first. Domesday Book

Brougham Castle, dating from the twelfth century.

makes no mention of any place, it being considered part of Scotland. Late in the eleventh century William Rufus took Carlisle from Dolfin, son of Gospatrick and brought in English farmers to make better use of the richer land. In the best Norman fashion the area was divided into baronies on both parts of the present border, and the castles were established; but only on the fringes of the Lake

District at Brougham, Kendal, Penrith, Millom, Egremont and Cockermouth. However, the border with Scotland was not finally settled. David I of Scotland took Cumbria back into Scotland in 1137. Twenty years later Malcolm IV of Scotland handed the territory back to Henry II, but the border and its clans were to remain a problem for centuries.

The great influence on the Lake District in the medieval period came with the establishment of the abbeys and their exploitation and husbandry of the countryside. Furness Abbey, the English Heritage building south of the national park between Dalton and Barrow (SD 218717), still standing to its original height, was founded by the order of Savigny but building on a grander scale began when the order merged with the Cistercians in 1147. The Cistercians made good use of their holdings. The vast woodlands of the Silurian hills provided fuel and timber for building and the making of utensils, furniture and tools, as well as providing venison and pannage for pigs. There were great pastures for sheep and cattle. The lakes provided fish. There was stone for the quarrying and mines to provide lead and iron. The wool trade was established.

The religious houses of Cumbria, like the castles,

Part of the ruins of Furness Abbey. The abbey had a great influence on the economic and social life of much of the Lake District.

The ruin of Calder Abbey in the west of the national park. Calder was a daughter abbey of Furness, twice sacked by the Scots and twice restored.

were built around the rim of the Lake District and there were few churches within its valleys. Crosthwaite church, at Keswick, however, was founded in the late twelfth century. Hawkshead's was an early thirteenth-century chapel as probably was St Martin's at Bowness. St Andrew's at Dacre has a late twelfth-century chancel, and St Michael's at Barton two miles east of Dacre has some fine Norman features.

Largely due to monastic management, the central Lake District in the twelfth and thirteenth centuries was being cleared of forest to extend the sheep pastures. There was a growing prosperity in the wool trade. Lower land was being drained. Populations grew, small settlements became hamlets; but there came a serious obstacle to further progress. The Border disputes and battles with Scotland were a constant drain on resources and brought worry and hardship for generations. Raids and counter-raids in the north were frequent. In 1138 it came to a head when Scots raiders got as far as Calder which was sacked. The monks fled and the abbey had to be recolonized by Furness Abbey five years later. There was another serious incursion in 1216, but after the English defeat at

Bannockburn the Scots twice raided as far as southern Lake District in 1316. This was so devastating that the papal tax on Furness Abbey which was assessed at £176 in 1291, was reduced to £13 6s 8d in 1318, yet there was another raid to come six years later when the abbey was forced to pay ransom.

As a defence of the Border, up to the sixteenth century, landlords' tenants, including the ecclesiastical, had written into tenancy agreements that they must equip themselves at their own expense, with arms, and horse and body armour, and that they must respond and report at an hour's notice 'upon warning given by fyring of a becon, post or proclamation by the Lord Warden of the Marches'. This service was not to the landlord, but to the Crown, the Lord Warden being the Crown's agent. To some this service gave privileged tenant rights by which they and their heirs held the land securely so long as they paid their landlord's rents and 'fines': a one-off payment on the death or change of a landlord.

The major Scots incursions were not the only worry. Cattle rustling by the Border clans was almost a way of life, though the inhabitants of the central Lake District may have escaped much attention as they might have been thought not worth robbing. The 'reivers' of the Border clans have been romanticized in the Border ballads. In fact they could be ruthless robbers, and they operated what we would now call a 'protection racket', and introduced a new word into the English language: 'black mail' (black rent). Some would call themselves Scots and English according to whichever seemed most profitable at the time.

There were other worries for the farmers working the rough land and the thin soils of the hills. Fortunes fluctuated considerably. There was always a market for wool, but the dreaded sheep 'murrain' (disease) would annihilate whole flocks. No doubt every farm had its arable field, though oats was the only grain crop that hill land would support, and if the season was a bad one it meant famine; for the crops of the wheat and barley growers in the better fringe areas would also be poor and the price to buyers high. Holdings were generally small. For most it was the barest of subsistence farming.

Throughout the medieval period some farmers and farm workers might have been only part-timers when local industry could offer some extra income. Mining and the local supporting industries which went with it offered one lift to the economy. Iron 'bloomeries' (crude hearths in wooded areas where ore was smelted with charcoal) were in use from the earliest times, though dating is difficult. Sites of these can be seen and identified by slag heaps, in scattered areas all over the district; for instance on the east shore of Coniston Water. The activity might explain the name 'Cinderdale' for the common by

The Coniston Valley seen from Tarn Hows. The valley was once a busy centre of the iron and charcoal industries.

Crummock Water.

Copper, lead and silver were also to be found. The earliest mines were opened in the Coniston Old Man area and had no doubt contributed to the wealth of Furness Abbey. Mining activity increased in Tudor times. Following promising prospecting in the sixteenth century, Keswick soon became a busy mining town. In 1564 the Company of Mines Royal was founded with powers to search for all metals, the Crown being eligible to receive a tenth of all gold, silver, and copper found. German mine experts were brought into Keswick in 1565 and colonized Derwent Island. They were not welcomed at first but later some married local girls and settled. Mines were opened in the nearby valleys, the most profitable being 'Goldscope' in the Newlands Valley. Water mills powered Keswick's furnace bellows. Ore was even brought in the long distance from the Coniston mines. Huge quantities of charcoal were needed and woods all over the Lake District were devastated. Peat was also dug and carted from a wide area. It is hard to imagine now: the hills about Derwent Water and Borrowdale bare of woods, smoke palls over Keswick and the noise of bellows and hammers. Nature heals industrial areas given time.

Ruin of the manager's house on the site of the eighteenth-century Duddon Furnace.

Not only copper, lead and iron were mined; but pure 'wad' or 'black lead' was found near Seathwaite. This mineral was so valued that an armed guard had to keep watch at the mine. Wad founded a Keswick industry which still survives: the making of lead pencils, although nowadays the graphite is imported. The tale is told at the Cumberland Pencil Museum in the town.

Mines were also opened behind Skiddaw and in the higher Ullswater Valley. At its peak the industry provided work for many hundreds of men, but by the last half of the seventeenth century there was a decline. However, the picture was patchy as metal prices fluctuated. For instance Brandlehow mine or 'Brandley' on the south-west shore of Derwent Water kept working intermittently up to the nineteenth century when a large water-wheel, and later a steam engine, were employed to pump water from the workings. Now only the birch-covered waste heaps give away its location. Greenside mine on the east side of Helvellyn was opened in the eighteenth century and was producing until 1962. The National Park Authority has acquired the site to try to establish grass and tree growth on the fell-side scars. Mining continued too on Coniston Old

Sheep gathered at Hartsop.

Man from the sixteenth century to the 1950s.

Mining undoubtedly helped the rural economy from the sixteenth century. Some farms might not have survived without the ancillary work the industry provided. However, there were social consequences. James Clarke, author of *Survey of the Lakes* in 1787, painted an exaggerated picture of the influence of mining immigrants:

> '. . . vice and poverty sit pictured in almost every countenance, and the rustic fireside is no longer the abode of peace – These fellows, who are in general the most abandoned, wicked, and profligate part of mankind no sooner settled here than they immediately began to propagate their vices among the innocent unsuspecting inhabitants. The farmer listened greedily to stories of places he had never seen – his daughters allured by promises, were seduced; even those who withstood promises, and were actually married, were, upon the stopping of the mines, deserted – and left to all the horrors of poverty and shame'.

(Nowadays, still concerned about the pressures on rural family life, we blame the television.)

Kendal's motto is 'Wool is my bread'. It bought the farmers' bread too and the big landowners their luxuries. 'Kendal Cotton' was a popular, cheap and durable woollen cloth. 'Kendal Green' was also popular. 'Three knaves in Kendal Green' are mentioned by Shakespeare (*Henry IV, Part 1*). Kendal was described by Camden, the Elizabethan historian, as 'a place famed for excellent clothing'.

The knitting of Kendal hose was one industry which continues today. The wool trade seemed to be at its best in the sixteenth century. The wool was usually spun at the farm, woven locally, then sent to be 'improved' (felted) under the hammers of one of the many water-powered fulling mills. They were everywhere. Grasmere had six in 1453. The abbeys organized the wool trade and confusion and some hardship must have been caused by their dissolution from 1536. The abbey holdings went into secular hands and the economy had to be re-shaped.

In 1603 the threat from the Border raiders ended when James VI of Scotland and I of England put down the troublesome families ruthlessly with mass hangings and transportations. (The rebellion of 1745 passed by the Lake District.) The seventeenth century saw an uprise in the economy. Later as mining declined quarrying took over and the building period began.

6 **Buildings and roads**

Before the seventeenth century the stone buildings
of the Lake District were churches and chapels; but
also significantly as in all the Border counties, there
were the defensive tower-houses, usually called
'pele towers' (though strictly speaking the pele or
peel refers to the walled defensive yard in which
they stood). These towers, owned by the wealthier
landowners as a defence against the Scottish raiders
usually date from the fourteenth century, the
building no doubt prompted by the Bruce
incursions after Bannockburn. The towers had walls
of between four feet and ten feet thick. They were
three storeys high with a vaulted store room, most
often doorless and lit only by narrow slits at ground
floor. Access to the first floor living quarters was by
a ladder which could be drawn up, or a stone
staircase, and through a heavy oak door protected
by an iron grill. The upper floor was a more airy
chamber. Above there were walkways behind
battlements. At warning of the approach of raiders,
possibly by beacon, the cattle would be hidden, and
the family and servants would retreat into the tower
until the raiders went away.

There are fewer of these towers within the central
Lake District compared with the vulnerable richer
areas around, but they can still be found in stages of
ruin or otherwise, for instance at Burneside,
Kentmere, Yanwath, Irton and Broughton. The best
preserved example is Dacre Castle north of
Ullswater (not open to the public).

In later more settled and prosperous times some
of these towers were incorporated by the wealthy
into extended comfortable residences. There are
some excellent examples. The gardens at
Muncaster Castle near Ravenglass, favoured by the
mild coastal climate, are magnificent, particularly at
rhododendron time; but the astonishing view from
its terrace, right up Eskdale to the Scafells, is
tremendous: positively Wagnerian. This is an idyllic
setting for a stately home and here it is built in the
blush-pink Eskdale granite and flanked with two
towers. In fact the tower at the south-west end is a
pele tower built in 1325. Salvin, the great

The fourteenth-century pele tower at Kentmere Hall.

nineteenth-century architect specializing in transforming castles into country homes, balanced the ancient tower with another new one at the north-west end of his new building. There are other examples of the very old tower being blended into the (relatively) new stately home which are also open to the public. Dalemain, built of the local limestone the colour of crushed blackberry, is north of Ullswater. Sizergh Castle (National Trust) and Levens Hall, are two others, just outside the national park on the A6 south of Kendal.

But the farmhouses before the seventeenth century were built of wood or clay and no signs remain. At the succession of James I in 1603 and the end of the Border troubles, an attempt was made to take away the old rights of tenure enjoyed by the local farmers, since the holders were no longer obliged to bear arms in service to the Crown. The proposal was violently opposed and there were law-suits and petitions. The decision of the King's Bench in 1625 upheld the tenants' rights regardless of their old obligations of service as their lands were 'estated of inheritance at the will of the lord, descendible from ancestor and heir according to the several customs of the several manors whereof

Wall End Farm, Langdale, with basically seventeenth- and eighteenth-century buildings, owned by the National Trust.

they are holden'.

The certainty of security encouraged more substantial rebuilding at a time when the economy had improved. The typical farmhouse was built 'back-side to wind' to a basic pattern with some variations, and consisted of two units: a crude 'down house' where the work was done, and a 'fire house' (or just 'house') living quarters, with a passage or 'hallan' dividing them. The front door led into the hallan. At the far end of the hallan, opposite doors led into the down house and into the fire house. The latter was entered by a short doorless passage, and immediately round the partition was the open hearth covered by a large hood under which it was possible to sit. The fire house was usually lit by two windows, but the hearth area also had its own small 'fire window', for the hearth, under the great hood, was the hub of the indoor activity. It had a disadvantage when it rained in that sooty blobs would descend down the chimney, which is why, some say, Cumbrian farmers wear their caps indoors! Other features of the house included built-in bread and spice cupboards.

Similarly the farm outbuildings, previously of wood or wattle, were rebuilt of stone during the

Working by the hearth in the light from the fire window. A painting by E M Nicholson, *c.* 1860.

same period. One feature of these might be an open 'spinning gallery' on the side. The two good examples with the latter are the much photographed Yew Tree Farm north of Coniston, and a barn opposite Town End, Troutbeck. Other examples can be spotted all over the district. Town End at Troutbeck (National Trust, NY 407023) reveals how an old farmhouse was improved by a relatively wealthy farmer in the eighteenth century. A new entrance was made and the hallan converted into a pantry. The down house became a kitchen. One fine detail of Town End is the typical home-carved oak panelling and furniture. A walk around Troutbeck village reveals some fine examples of vernacular architecture of the seventeenth to the nineteenth centuries. The heavy looking cylindrical chimneys are a feature of this period. Coniston Hall, on the west side of Coniston Water, looks from a distance like an old funnelled steamship.

At this time too some of the valley chapels, probably previously built of wood, were rebuilt in stone; while others in disrepair were restored. Grasmere's church is a fascinating hotch-potch of styles, but owes much to the sixteenth, seventeenth and eighteenth centuries. Hawkshead's church is of

the sixteenth and seventeenth centuries. Some of the
chapels were built like the farm barns. A fascinating
jewel of an example is St Anthony's of Cartmel Fell
(SD 417881). The old chapel at Martindale
(NY 434184) is another. There is also the tiny church
at Wasdale Head, its timbers reputedly claimed
from a shipwreck. Wythburn church, all that
remains of the village 'drowned' by Thirlmere

Hawkshead church.

Reservoir, is another (NY 325136).

There was another kind of building in the
eighteenth and nineteenth centuries which was to
make a profound impact on the landscape. Before
then much of the land was completely open with all
inhabitants having common rights. There were field
and park walls, some of them monastic boundaries
and quite old. Others by common agreement fenced
off stock from arable land, and others, such as the
enormously thick walls at Wasdale Head, were
largely built as a convenient way of ridding the
fields of stones. Between 1760 and 1850, however,
wall building was boosted by the Enclosure Acts
and the incentives to improve agriculture,
particularly because of the Napoleonic wars when
food prices were high. As in other areas of Britain,
while being of some benefit to agriculture, the
enclosures benefited the wealthier farmers and the
big landowners, but sometimes impoverished the
small men. Under the Act of 1801 Commissioners
were empowered to conduct surveys and apportion
common land and open fields between petitioners
and those holding old common rights. The recipient
of an award had to build his own enclosure by an
agreed date in a detailed specific manner as to

Drystone walls on
Loughrigg Fell.

height and method. If a recipient could not afford to do this he was forced to lose his ancient rights and sell. Itinerant wallers were employed and paid by the rood. Many worked from dawn to dusk, sleeping where they finished each day's work. The stone had first to be 'won' from the nearest outcrop to hand.

The walls soar up the heights occasionally over seemingly impossible places. Many fell-sides look as if they have been spread with a giant net. Some walls testify to the amazing skill of their builders, for although the rock is rough and comes in all shapes, the wall faces are flush. A drystone wall is really two walls leaning against each other, broad-based and narrow-topped, with a centre of small stones or 'heartings'. At two or three levels 'throughs', long stones, go from front to back and lock the walls together. The top is finished with 'cams', stones laid almost vertically and tight together to keep out the weather. Their strength is that as the land 'creeps' the walls settle and remain standing, where cemented walls would crack and develop hollows. Some walls show the strength of the builders for they incorporate colossal rocks which would not only have to be lifted in place, but turned around to sit firmly. All are worth examination. The geologist wishing to determine the type of local rock need look no further. For a naturalist they are a habitat for lichens and ferns and small animals. Their preservation as a fence and a landscape feature, when skilled hands are rare, is a cause for concern.

Up to the eighteenth century conditions for the hill farmer continued to be harsh. His stock might only consist of twenty to forty sheep, two horses, ten cows and a bull. Many settlements had common fields with a rota system of overseeing them, and strict rules as to when, where, and what grazing should be allowed. The local sheep breed, seen nowhere else, was the 'Herdwick', a handsome little animal still favoured by many farmers to this day as it is able to withstand the harshest conditions on the fells. There are two traditional theories of its origins: the first that the animals were beached from a wrecked ship of the Spanish Armada, which is not likely; the second is that they were brought over by the Viking settlers, which is possible. The hill farmers' sheep, as they are to this day, were 'hefted': bred on, and accustomed to their home fell and disinclined to wander off it. The sheep go with the farm as it changes hands. The Herdwicks were the only sheep until the larger landowners began experimenting with other breeds from the late eighteenth century.

The increased building of enclosures made a new movement possible, from the latter half of the eighteenth to the first half of the nineteenth century, to improve the land and stock. The fertility of the acid soil of the 'town fields', now walled off into individual strips, was improved by the application

Complicated wall patterns in a Lake District valley.

of lime. Lime too was used for the first time, with heavy applications of manure, to improve the farms' nearer 'inbye' land. Lime was also applied to the enclosed 'intake' land (second-class land 'taken in' from the nearby lower fells). Wet land was drained using tiles as well as slates. On the open fell slopes heather and heath were cut and burned together with the acid humus below. Where possible this land was ploughed afterwards and limed, and as a result new larger areas of pasture were brought into use, and the stocking levels increased. So the landscape saw change. In the valleys there were new straggling wall patterns everywhere. Wet land which had once been covered with alders, willows and rushes, became pasture. What had been rough fell sides were tamed. Enclosed fields shone with a new bright green. Only the large areas of higher common fell land remained unaltered. The characteristic shape of the landscape remained the same as ever; but the colours and textures changed to produce the mild dales scenes that we can see today.

The roads before the latter half of the eighteenth century were, to say the least, somewhat rough and often hard to find. The larger lakes were much used as highways from early times. (Hence the now isolated little chapel on the shore by Mirehouse, Bassenthwaite.) The way into the district from the south was by Lancaster and across the sands of Morecambe Bay at low tide. For this purpose it was advisable to use the local guide, at first probably a monastic one, latterly an appointee of the Duchy of Lancaster. (Indeed the way is still a public road. The guide lives at Kents Bank and hundreds walk the route with him annually.) The trick is knowing where there are quicksands and where the River Kent is at its shallowest. Over the centuries many have perished in the crossing. Memorials in Cartmel Priory church testify to the dangers. It is said that a party at Kents Bank would watch the sands and if they saw someone crossing at the wrong time for the tide, which rushes in at a notoriously speedy rate, they would cast lots as to who would have his pack, his saddle, or his coat. When Turner visited the Lakes he painted two evocative pictures of parties crossing the sands.

Much of the transport into the eighteenth century was by packhorse. Trains of ponies from Kendal traversed the fells on tracks now only used by fell walkers; and alas the worse for wear from generations of neglect, such as the route by

Old sign at Cartmel, indicating the routes across Morecambe Bay.

Langdale and Rossett Gill and Styhead to Wasdale and Borrowdale, and the way to Mardale via Longsleddale and Gatescarth Pass. But packhorse trains also went to York, Durham, and London. However after 1750 there were a number of Turnpike Acts. Turnpike companies were given powers to improve roads, erect toll bars and take payment from travellers. As roads improved traffic increased. The first tourists arrived by stage coach and post chaise to found the Lake District's new major industry.

Kirkstone Pass, the highest road in the national park.

7 **The first tourists**

It is a calm fine day in autumn. It is only a modest height but you struggle to the summit breathless from the final very steep ascent among larch trees, through the mounds and ditches of an ancient hill-fort, on to a rocky plateau. You are on a natural platform in the middle of a great amphitheatre. Around you the high flanking crags and hills of Borrowdale; King How and Grange Fell are aflare with the colours of autumn: brown, red, yellow and gold. To the north the best view of scarcely rippled Derwent Water, the whole splendid tree-clad vale before you, and behind it the great sprawl of Skiddaw and Blencathra. Turn around and you see above through the frondose clouds of autumn trees hanging to the sides of the corridor of upper Borrowdale, beyond to the wilderness of fells, to Great Gable and the Scafells. To the east the first

Grasmere, Father West's preferred viewpoint.

snows of autumn touch the top of Helvellyn. This sublime place is 'Station IV' of Keswick.

Station? The viewing 'stations' of Father West, a Jesuit priest, were the beginnings of popular tourism in the Lake District, for it was he who wrote the first guide-book in 1778. It was a best seller. The market for the book was waiting, for the District had already been painted, written and talked about for some time. Father West, who was in post at Dalton in Furness at the time, knew this well enough and starts the book:

> 'Since persons of genius, taste, and observation began to make the tour of their own country and to give such pleasing accounts of the natural history, and improving state of the northern parts of the kingdom, the spirit of visiting them has diffused itself among the curious of all ranks.
>
> Particularly the taste for [painting] ... – induces many to visit the Lakes – there to contemplate in Alpine scenery, finished in nature's highest tints, the pastoral and rural landscape – the soft, the rude, the romantic and the sublime of which perhaps like instance can no where be found assembled in so small a tract of country.'

So the guide takes the reader to thirteen lakes and eleven villages and towns (including Lancaster), suggesting the best stations, twenty-one of them, and describing the views. Some are now difficult to locate, but obvious ones can be enjoyed today. Belle Isle, north and south, Latrigg above Keswick (NY 279247), Broadness by Bassenthwaite (NY 218296). An important one by Windermere was Station I on the west shore above the ferry (SD 386956). Here in 1799 when the land was in the ownership of the then Ferry Hotel, a 'pleasure house' was built to help viewers better appreciate the scene. The ruin is now in the care of the National Trust. Of Station IV Keswick (Castle Crag) West states 'The views here taken in the glass, when the sun shines, are amazingly fine'. The 'glass' was not a sip of brandy from the tourist's hip-flask, but a 'Claude Glass'. It came in several forms but normally it was a slightly concave mirror in a handsome frame. The viewer would stand with his back to the scene, holding the glass up to see it all reduced to a framed landscape suggestive of a painting by the famous artist Claude Lorraine (1600–82).

The northern reaches of Windermere, and the central fells, from Orrest Head viewpoint, above Windermere town.

The 'persons of genius, taste, and observation' discovered the Lake District in the eighteenth century because of a coming together of several circumstances. Firstly there was the romantic mood of the times. The socially privileged have oft times pretended that they wanted to be shepherds and shepherdesses.

> 'O God! Methinks it were a happy life
> To be no better than a homely swain;
> to sit upon a hill, as I do now. –
> To carve out dials quaintly point to point.
> Oh what a life were this! How sweet! How lovely!
> Gives not the hawthorn bush a sweeter shade
> To shepherds looking on their silly sheep,
> Than doth a rich embroidered canopy
> To kings . . . ?'

So, according to Shakespeare, Henry VI felt when he was having a bad time. (Nowadays the shepherd is not the romantic figure he was; if the national parks' correspondence is anything to go by he seems to have been superseded by the national park ranger.)

In the second half of the eighteenth century in Britain there was a more favourable economic

Ullswater at Glenridding.

climate. Wealth and leisure were more widely enjoyed. The scare of the '45 rebellion had receded and there was a sense of security. For a broader-based aristocracy, wealth came more easily and there was not so much concern with the sordid task of making more and more money. That came in the following century. There was a desire to be surrounded with beautiful things which led to an interest in collecting works of art. It was an elegant age. It was a flowering time of art and literature and good taste when fine architecture and craftsmanship were esteemed. The Grand Tour had introduced many to European painting, and at this time notably the landscapes of the Rome school including those of Claude Lorraine. His six books *Libri di Verità*, with small copies of his pictures, helped to set a fashion, with landscape being the main theme of the painting (with obligatory foreground shepherds and shepherdesses), rather than as a background to a nobleman's portrait, or some religious or mythological event. The landscapes of Claude, Salvator Rosa and Poussin were much discussed and written about in Britain if not always well seen. Landscape became something to study, evaluate, and admire.

Concurrently there was a new philosophy which

lifted the romantic vision of the countryside to a slightly higher plain. It was perhaps stimulated by the works of Jean-Jacques Rousseau. There grew a belief in the essential beauty and innocence of things natural.

The quest for beautiful landscape in Britain was also caused to some extent by the unsettled state of Europe, which depressed the desire for the Grand Tour; and there was an awakening patriotism. Then there was the long-needed improvement in the country roads that West refers to. Finally there were some better maps that no gentlemen's libraries could be without. Notably the Society of Arts offered a bonus of £100 for new one inch to the mile maps based on surveys. As a result a Westmorland map was produced by Thomas Jeffreys in 1770; Cumberland by Hodskinson and Donald in 1774; Lancashire by Yates in 1786.

When the quest took flight the publication of a letter by a Dr John Brown to Lord Lyttleton (*c.*1750) brought attention to the Lakes. Dr Brown described the 'Vale and Lake of Keswick' with enthusiasm. He is impressed by the '*horror* of the rugged cliffs' and the '*dreadful* heights'; both adjectives being fashionable in landscape descriptions but no matter: it was an admirable piece of composition praised later by Wordsworth and it was much read. West refers to it in his guide; his later editions reproduced the letter in full.

The poet Thomas Gray now enters the scene. It is quite probable that he had read Dr Brown's letter as he had done the Grand Tour with Horace Walpole, one of Lord Lyttleton's circle. Gray had already been impressed by the Alps. He was also impressed by a ten-day stay in the Lakes in 1769. His account of it in a letter to a friend (posthumously published in 1775) had a large readership. Fell walkers today can smile incredulously at his description of Styhead, the M1 of today's fell routes from Seathwaite, as a 'dreadful road – for *some weeks in the year* passable to Dalesmen.' But his description of his descent from Dunmail to the vale of Grasmere is well quoted and approved of by all romanticizers of the rural scene: 'not a single red tile, no gentlemen's flaring house, or garden walls, break in upon the repose of this little unsuspecting paradise; but all is peace, rusticity, and happy poverty, in its neatest and most becoming attire'.

In 1772 from Surrey came William Gilpin, a guide-book writer, and clergyman of another persuasion, who was also a fairly well-to-do retired schoolmaster. In 1786 he published his book *Observations relative to Picturesque Beauty made in the year 1772 on a tour through England more particularly the mountainous parts of Cumberland and Westmorland.* The title suggests the style, but this too made a very significant contribution to the tourist attraction of the Lakes. His book laid down the ground rules for admiring the landscape 'for the man of taste to pursue the beauties of nature'; though in Gilpin's evaluations nature very often does not pass the test. It perhaps lacks composition, a mountain in the wrong place, a poor foreground. He is not suggesting how the scene should be painted, but how it should be looked at. His work was an obvious target for later satires.

Meanwhile 'persons of genius and taste', amateur and professional, were visiting in greater numbers, sketching, painting, writing and discussing. Father West's stations must have been thronged at times with artists' easels, stools, picnic baskets, and elegant people discussing the merits of the scene as they stared at it in their Claude glasses. The many paintings, drawings, engravings, of the Lake District by fine artists are scattered through art galleries all over Britain. Most say more about the artists or the fashion of the times than about the real Lake District, but many are masterpieces.

J M W Turner did his first tour of the north of England in 1797 at the age of twenty-two. He was to return and make a number of paintings. 'Morning amongst the Coniston Fells' in the Tate, shows his genius. William Green, a Manchester surveyor, who was encouraged to become an artist by Father West, settled in Ambleside in 1800 and had a formidable output of engravings and drawings. He made a living from the sale of prints and was much praised by Wordsworth. His skill was in the finer detail of rocks and trees. Sir George Beaumont (1753 – 1827) was a frequent visitor and took a house at Brathay, Ambleside. He was a patron as much as an artist and belonged to a circle of contemporary artists and encouraged some to visit the Lakes. He became a close friend of Wordsworth who relied upon him absolutely for his opinions on art.

John Constable visited the Lakes in 1806, staying with his friend and gifted amateur artist, John Harden at Brathay Hall. He made some seventy sketches and water colours. In spite of writing on one drawing 'the finest scenery that ever was', he did not return to the Lakes, confessing to a friend that he found mountains oppressive.

Opposite 'Morning amongst the Coniston Fells' by JMW Turner.

Rothay Bridge near Ambleside. A drawing by William Green.

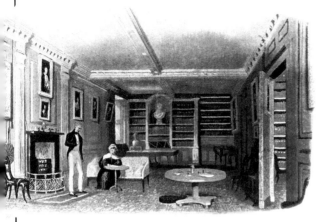

'Room at Rydal Mount', with William and Mary Wordsworth; an engraving by William Westall.

Gainsborough spent some time in the Lake District late in his career in 1783, making a number of drawings and paintings. Prolific artist J C Ibbetson (1759–1817) married a local girl and lived in the Lake District for eleven years at Ambleside and Troutbeck. He had a rare sense of humour. He painted the original amusing inn sign at the Mortal Man in Troutbeck (NY 411035). Another prolific artist in water colours and engravings was William Westall (1781–1850). He was much admired by Southey, who had him illustrate some literary work, and Wordsworth who consented to him doing an engraving of the long parlour at Rydal Mount, with the figures of himself and his wife.

The interest in the romantic picturesque attracted a great deal of building in this style by local landowners and 'offcomers'. The round house on Belle Isle, the large island by Bowness, is a fine example of one built in 1774 for purely picturesque reasons. Its builder, a Mr English, was much criticised for his doubtful taste, but in 1789 the house was acquired by the Curwen family, whose fortunes had been lately increased by coal mining, and J C Curwen landscaped the garden and planted much of the beautiful woodland on the west side of Windermere. (House open to the public.) One Joseph Pocklington went to extremes on Derwent Water. On Derwent Island in 1778 he built, not only a house, but a mock church, fort and battery complete with cannons, and a 'Druids' Circle', and used the island as a centre for extravagant regattas. In 1787 he built 'Barrow Cascade House', now Borrowdale Youth Hostel, and a cottage at Bowder Stone where he employed an old lady as a guide. Regretfully the finest most extravagant example of 1806, Lowther Castle (NY 522239) has now only the façade to show. The building was too costly to maintain. There are other examples of the period's buildings throughout the district. Some are now hotels, such as Storrs Hall (1808) near Bowness; its 'temple' on the lake shore is now owned by the National Trust. Belmount, near Hawkshead is c.1790.

Wordsworth regretted the bad taste of some of the builders. He came to Dove Cottage at Grasmere in 1799 and his best-selling *Guide to the Lakes* was published in 1810. It owes something to Father West even in the introductory passage which flatters the intended reader (so assuring instant sale). West referred to 'persons of genius, taste and observation' with his book 'furnishing the traveller with a guide'. And Wordsworth wrote: 'In preparing this manual it was the author's principal wish to furnish a Guide or Companion for the Minds of Persons of Taste –'. However Wordsworth's guide-book broke a lot of new ground and is a best-seller to this day.

William Wordsworth was born in a house on Cockermouth's main street in 1770, educated as a boy at Hawkshead Grammar School, moved much later to a cottage at Town End, Grasmere, later called Dove Cottage; and finally lived at Rydal Mount. All these places are preserved and open to the public and visited by Wordsworth enthusiasts from all over the world. Considering his literary output inevitably some of Wordsworth's works must be trite. But it was when he settled at Dove Cottage with his sister Dorothy, from 1799 to 1808, that he was at the height of his powers and wrote some of the greatest poetry in the English language; much inspired by his talented sister. 'She gave me eyes. She gave me ears.' She also gave him words and whole lines, often from her journal; and she gave him 'daffodils'. Maybe if William knew how so many schoolchildren later might be satiated and possibly nauseated by his dancing daffodils, maybe even put off poetry for life, he would have regretted writing it. Could he who wrote that simple poem have composed the profoundly moving 'Ode to Intimations of Immortality'? But at least it took him two years to finish that. Among the other great works composed at Dove Cottage were the *Prelude* (obligatory reading for Lakes connoisseurs), the *Lyrical Ballads*, miscellaneous sonnets, 'The Solitary Reaper', 'The Rainbow', some of the 'Lucy' poems, and others.

Daffodils in Dora's Field, Rydal. These were planted by William Wordsworth for his daughter, and the area is owned by the National Trust.

Dorothy's journal of the days at Dove Cottage is of notable literary merit. It seems likely that if she had been less devoted and generous with her ideas to William as she was, she could have been a fine poet in her own right. Dove Cottage and its museum should be visited by all who value the poet's unique contribution to English literature, and those interested in the Wordsworth period (NY 342070).

William brought his bride, Mary Hutchinson, a childhood friend, to Dove Cottage in 1802. She gave him three children and when she was expecting a fourth the little cottage became too crowded for comfort and they moved to Allan Bank in Grasmere before eventually moving to Rydal Mount.

Wordsworth's close friendship and collaboration with ST Coleridge is well known. Before the Dove Cottage period the two spent a year together in Somerset, walking the Quantock hills. Coleridge had a brilliant mind and it was from their discussions that Wordsworth's thoughts on poetry took direction. Coleridge also obtained inspiration from William, and he too took some ideas and images from the generous Dorothy. It was in the Somerset period that Coleridge was encouraged to write 'The Ancient Mariner'. It was therefore not surprising that Coleridge followed the Wordsworths to the Lakes in 1800, renting a part of Greta Hall at Keswick (now part of a school). The five-hour walk between the two friends was as nothing to them. Coleridge wrote an entertaining account of *A Tour in the Lake Country* in 1802. His description of his dangerous descent of Scafell down the crags on the Eskdale side is quite hair-raising (Coleridge records that it raised heat-lumps on him). The epic should go down in the annals of mountaineering!

Coleridge had married the sister-in-law of Robert Southey, and in 1803 the Southeys also moved to Greta Hall for a stay. As it happened the 'stay' was for the rest of the forty years of Southey's life. Southey's energy and competence as a writer brought sufficient income to support his family, and Coleridge's; for Coleridge, crippled in mind and body by an addiction to opium, began a decline. He left for Malta for his health's sake in 1804, returned a year later, but, his relationship with Wordsworth estranged, left the Lakes for good in 1810.

Southey's works are largely forgotten apart perhaps from 'After Blenheim', 'The Holly Tree', 'The Scholar', and 'The Life of Nelson'; but his delightful poem, written for children, about the 'Cataract of Lodore' is a rare treat. Starting slowly at its source the metre speeds up to the final fall:

> 'Pouring and roaring.
> And waving and raving,
> And tossing and crossing . . .'

Southey became Poet Laureate in 1813. At his death in 1843 Wordsworth wrote his memorial which is in Crosthwaite church at Keswick.

Literary visitors to the Lakes were many. Charles Lamb came to visit his friend Coleridge in 1802 and climbed Skiddaw. When the Wordsworths were at Dove Cottage they were visited by Thomas de Quincey who hero-worshipped the bard. He was scared off his first attempt to visit when he stood on Father West's viewpoint at Red Bank and saw Dove Cottage in the distance. Coleridge's 'Ancient Mariner' and Wordsworth's *Lyrical Ballads* had an effect on De Quincey 'an absolute revelation of untrodden worlds, teeming with power and beauty'.' Eventually he joined the Wordsworth circle and when the bard and his family left Dove Cottage he took the lease.

De Quincey was a friendly scholarly character who filled the cottage with books and struggled to

repay debts. His relationship with the Wordsworths became strained; his addiction to opium was one obstacle; another was his marriage to a village girl, Margaret Simpson, for she was socially unacceptable. In fact the marriage was a success. His home was Dove Cottage for two decades. His *Confessions of an Opium Eater* as a series of instalments in the London Magazine in 1821 established his literary reputation. His 'Recollections of the Lake Poets', written first as a series of articles in Tait's Edinburgh Magazine (1834–40) shows great depth and sympathetic insight. It is also amusing without being cruel. He comments on William's inelegant legs, but which he calculated had strode over 180,000 English miles. Southey 'wore pretty constantly a short jacket and pantaloons, and had much the air of a Tyrolese mountaineer'.

John Keats was an enthusiastic visitor to the Lakes and climbed Skiddaw. Percy Bysshe Shelley stayed with his young bride in Keswick for several months during 1811–12. Charles Dickens and Wilkie Collins struggled up Carrock Fell in 1851.

Sir Walter Scott visited the Wordsworths at Town End and returned to the Lake District several times. Both *Guy Mannering* and *Redgauntlet* have

Dove Cottage at Grasmere, home of the Wordsworths when William was at the height of his powers. It is open to the public.

Cumbrian settings. He wrote a poem about Gough, a walker killed on Helvellyn and guarded by his faithful dog for several months. 'The Bridal of Triermain' poem is set in St Johns in the Vale; the ghostly castle – there at one moment with towers, turrets, battlements and buttresses, and the next melting into crags – is Castle Rock, much enjoyed by rock climbers today who, alas, do not on completing the ascent meet with a 'band of damsels fair', though with the amount of climbing-aid ironmongery carried nowadays the damsels' attention might be welcome:

> 'A hundred lovely hands assail
> The bucklers of the monarch's mail,
> And busy laboured to unhasp
> Rivet of steel and iron clasp.'

In the Wordsworth circle was one John Wilson who was 'Christopher North' of Blackwoods Magazine and Professor of Moral Philosophy and Political Economy at Edinburgh. He was a man that the ordinary mortal could easily learn to hate, for he knew everyone and was good at everything, scholar, writer, organizer, but also an athlete, enjoying the local sports, beating the local strong men at wrestling. His literary style was often over sentimental, with occasional flashes of inspiration. It had a following.

Harriet Martineau (1802–76), a radical social reformer, political economist and prolific author, settled in Ambleside in 1845 and had a house built for her, and explored the area, largely on foot. Her excellent book *A Description of the English Lakes* (1858) was well received. As should be expected from a social reformer she did not see the local people as romantic figures in a landscape enjoying the 'happy poverty'. Of some of the communities she writes: 'The unhealthiness of many settlements is no less a shame than a curse, for the fault is in Man, not in Nature. Nature has fully done her part in providing rock for foundations, the purest air, and the amplest supply of running water; yet the people live – as we are apt to pity the poor of the metropolis for living – in stench, huddled together in cabins, and almost without water. The wilfulness of this makes the fact almost incredible; but the fact is so.' Such was her standing that she had distinguished visitors knocking on her door including John Bright, Charlotte Brontë, Matthew Arnold, Ralph Waldo Emerson, and Mary Ann Evans (George Eliot).

John Ruskin, art critic and artist, author and philosopher, settled at Brantwood on the east side of Coniston Water in 1871 where he was a revered and respected figure until he died, slightly but harmlessly mad, in 1900. Ruskin enthusiasts from all over the world visit the house with its superb outlook over Coniston Water (SD 313959) and the Ruskin Museum in the village. W G Collingwood was Ruskin's secretary. His books *The Lake Counties* (1902) and *Lake District History* contained much original research and are eminently readable.

The east shore of Coniston Water looking towards the Coniston Old Man range.

On the east shore of Bassenthwaite Lake at Mirehouse (open to the public) lived James Spedding, a native academic who spent years writing *The Life and Letters of Francis Bacon*. He had three good friends who enjoyed visiting him: Edward Fitzgerald, Thomas Carlyle, and Alfred Lord Tennyson. Tennyson was much taken by the place and his description in 'Idylls of the King' of the carrying off of Arthur's body in the ghostly barge, and the throwing of the sword Excalibur was inspired by his lake-side walks and the nearby lake-side chapel. A memorial stone marks the spot at Mirehouse shore (NY 226284):

'And in the moon athwart the place of tombs

Where lay the mighty bones of ancient men,
Old knights, and over them the sea-wind sang
Shrill, chill, with flakes of foam. He, stepping
down
By zig-zag path and juts of pointed rock,
Came on the shining levels of the lake.
Then drew he forth the brand Excalibur . . .

Bassenthwaite from the
Mirehouse shore.

Sir Hugh Walpole (1884–1941) the novelist, bought
Brackenburn overlooking Derwent Water in 1923
and wrote the popular Lake District novels *Rogue
Herries*, *Vanessa*, *The Fortress*, and *Judith Paris*.
The settings are authentic. Judith Paris is placed in
Watendlath, and Walpole followers seek out her
home there.

Beatrix Potter (1866–1943) was more artist than
author, but her 'Peter Rabbit' books have entranced
children for over eighty years. All her illustrations
were painted from local scenes. Her house at Hill
Top, Near Sawrey, near Hawkshead (National Trust)
attracts thousands of visitors annually, mainly adults
seeking nostalgic reminders of childhood.

This century has seen an enormous flow of books
and they come unabated. It is hardly possible to list
the notable ones. Writers currently with homes in
the Lake District area include Melvyn Bragg, Hunter
Davies, author and mountaineer Chris Bonington,
and the poet-author Norman Nicholson (born in
1914). Nicholson's poetry is well acclaimed, but his
books *The Lakers*, *Portrait of the Lakes*, *Greater
Lakeland*, *Cumberland and Westmorland*, are
among the best ever written about the Lake District.

8 The climate and natural history

When asked about the climate of the Lake District by a visitor a farmer was heard to answer 'Climate? We have nowt o'that here – just weather.' Wordsworth, deprecating Father West's recommendation in his *Guide* for July and August visits states:

> '[An] objection is rainy weather, setting in sometimes at this period with a vigour and continuing with a perseverance that may remind the disappointed and dejected traveller of those deluges of rain which fall among the Abyssinian mountains, for the annual supply of the Nile'.

Wordsworth may have had no knowledge of Africa, but his Lake District observation was not unfounded. In common with the rest of the country July and August can be cloudy. August sales of waterproofs keep some local trade alive, for that month takes an average of around nine per cent of the annual rainfall. May and June are normally the dryest months. Normally? The Lake District has

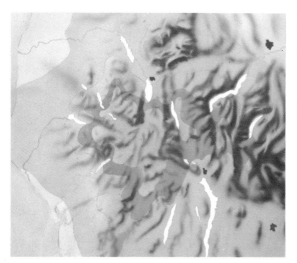

Inches	mm
Over 40 –	1016
Over 60 –	1524
Over 80 –	2032
Over 100 –	2540

Simplified map of the Lake District showing rainfall patterns.

suffered from August droughts and June floods. Droughts are not at all uncommon as farm and rural residents without mains water supplies know to their cost. With high Pennines to the east and Scottish hills to the north the area is dry and sunny with the wind in the north east. Winds from that quarter average about ninety days each year.

Every schoolchild used to be told (are they still?) that Seathwaite in the Lake District is the wettest place in England with an annual soaking of about 131 in; but fells around the Scafells might take between 150 in to 180 in. The rain is mainly caused by moist air moving in from the Atlantic to the south-west expanding and cooling as it is forced over the mountains. With converging air streams pushing through the configurations of the fells there are high averages of cloud cover and rain not only on the Scafells but on the Langdale, Hellvellyn, and Fairfield ranges. However, away from the effects of the mountains the rainfall is surprisingly less. From Seathwaite with its 131 in, Rosthwaite, down valley by only a little more than two miles has 100 in Grange in another two miles 90 in and in another three and a half miles Keswick has 57 in. The decline continues north east; Penrith has only about 35 in. Similarly while the high Langdale Fells might have around 170 in, twelve miles away at Windermere it is 60 in.

The number of wet days in the Lake District, apart from the high fells, is no greater than in most parts of England. The higher rainfall figures mean that when it does rain, it is rather heavier. The contrast is marked again. Light July rain falling in Borrowdale may not inconvenience the waterproofed valley walker; but on Great Gable the fell walker could be battling with 'horizontal stair rods', a gale-blown deluge, and heaven help him if he is not well equipped to face it.

The Lake District climate is dominated by the Atlantic air currents and the Gulf Stream. Overall that means that the winter temperatures are mild – Keswick's average January temperature (4°C/39°F) compares with London and Edinburgh and Grange over Sands by Morecambe Bay compares with the south coast of England. But the summers are cooler.

The district is a disappointment to skiers. Snow usually comes to Britain from the north and east, and again because of its sheltered position from these quarters the area remains relatively unscathed while other parts of the country are being snow-ploughed. On average, Keswick and Ambleside

Stormy weather brewing over Derwent Water.

Coniston Water shore at Old Brown Howe in winter, a national park picnic area.

have about twelve days of snow cover each year. By contrast the fell summit areas not exposed to the sun or thawing south westerlies may stay covered for 110 days. Snow drifts sometimes linger into June and July in north-eastern hollows. The contrasting snow cover on the eastern exposures compared with the west can often be seen. High Street and Helvellyn can have a fair summit covering while the Scafells' cover is thin or even non-existent. Wrynose Pass can be blocked by drifts, while its western neighbour, Hardknott, remains open.

As far as the weather is concerned a holiday anywhere in Britain is a gamble. National parks are for well equipped open-air people who do not normally bother too much about such things, but enjoy, not only the clear bright weather, but also the shifting cloud shadows, the apocalyptic sight of sunshine bursting through the mist, leaf colours rippled by the wind, torrents and crashing waterfalls, the view suddenly breaking from obscurity. As Wordsworth again says in his *Guide*: 'After all, it is upon the *mind* which a traveller brings along with him that his acquisition, whether of pleasure or profit, must principally depend'. If it all gets too much there could be the hospitality of a country pub, and with luck traditional rum-butter and fresh scones.

During the severe flooding in the Langdale in 1962 the long period of torrential rain saturated a terrace area of moss and peat over 2,000 feet up on a fell side to such an extent that it became a floating mass of the consistency of thick porridge. As fell walkers watched through the shrouds of rain they were amazed to see it beginning to quake. Then a barrier of rock detritus holding the whole area in place suddenly burst under the enormous pressure and the whole cascaded down the fell side in a great black wave. A walk around the eroded area some time afterwards revealed the remains of blackened tree roots: Scots pine, and some hardly identifiable broad-leaves, possibly birch, which had presumably been preserved deep in the peat. Pieces of old tree root occasionally surface elsewhere on the high fells up to 2,500 feet. Until extensive human colonization three to four thousand years ago the greater parts of the fells were covered with forest of pine, oak and birch with alder in the wet areas. It lingered on in many areas even when the early hill farmers made clearances with axe and fire. But the decline had to continue as demand grew for building timber, fuel, and later for

charcoal for the smelting furnaces. There was no
chance of the tree cover regenerating naturally for
any seedlings were eaten by sheep. A few thin
remnants of the high-level forest remain. An area of
straggly oak-wood 1,000 to 1,500 feet up at
Keskadale in the Newlands Valley might be such a
relic. On some of the high volcanic cliffs out of reach
of grazing sheep, trees seem to grow miraculously
out of the rock, their roots penetrating the clefts:
oak, holly, ash, birch, rowan and juniper. There are
other remnants in the gills (deep ravines) again out
of reach of sheep. Surveys made in the 1980s
revealed that the gills held typically woodland flora
clinging to the sides of the ravines. Some gills are
listed as Sites of Special Scientific Interest. It is likely
more will be made so. There is a concern that the
new sport of 'gill scrambling' might cause some
damage, but if the rules of the game are observed,
keeping participants to the solid rock, there is no
threat.

Now, to the delight of the freedom seekers, the
fells are open to the sky, apparently as they were
made by the cataclysmic events in the morning of
time. But not quite as naked. The summits are hostile
to most plant communities. They can freeze in the
night and burn in the radiation of the sun during the
day. They can be soaked by fog and rain at one
moment then blown dry by gales in the next. Any
soil there is acid, thin, and unstable. Yet amazingly
the mosses flourish; wavy hair moss, alpine club
moss, and several lichens and liverworts.

Below the summit the fell sides are nowhere
nearly as rich in alpine vegetation as one would
find, say, on the friable lime-rich mica-schists of the

View from the Scafells to
Wast Water.

Central Scottish Highlands. In the Borrowdale Volcanics the minerals are locked hard in the rock and are only released by frost and water action in the gills, and in wet 'flushes' where water wells to the surface. The east-facing coves, such as those on Helvellyn, on rocks and ledges inaccessible to sheep (and sometimes dangerous to man!) offer the largest number of alpine, moorland and woodland species.

Animals on the summits (apart from the odd groups of Homo Sapiens Alpina) are rare. There are bank voles by the summit shelters. Would they survive without the walkers' sandwich fragments? And how did they get there? Snow buntings and dotterels are welcome winter visitors.

Below the summit the cliffs are home to some of our more interesting birds. The ravens reign; masters of the air currents, they never quit the crags even in the depths of winter and they breed during the snows of March. The voice of the raven is sometimes the only sound to break the mountain silence. Peregrine falcons speed back to investigate the crags in March. Sometimes they share a cliff with ravens. In the 1950s they were scarce, for at that time successful breeding was prevented when they took prey which had ingested pesticides. The withdrawal of some pesticides has meant a recovery and now the national park is a major European breeding area for the species. The amazing sight – and sound – as they 'stoop' on their prey is now less rare. Sadly some depredations are made by human nest raiders, even though sites are watched; but rock climbers, who could easily disturb the birds at the critical nesting time, are now sufficiently concerned to give the sites a wide berth.

The exciting happening since the early 1960s is the return of the golden eagle after an absence from the Lake District of two centuries. There has been a successful breeding of one pair over some years. The nest site has been guarded by wardens of the Royal Society for the Protection of Birds, with some support from the National Park Authority. The birds' future seems promising.

Lower down the slopes life is more abundant. Britain's largest animal, the red deer, lives on in the eastern fells. The Martindale herds are animals which have adapted from an open woodland habitat to the often harsh conditions on the mountains. In winter they can sometimes be seen on the fell sides east of upper Ullswater. Stag roaring at the rut is one of the most exciting sounds of quiet autumn.

Golden eagle.

Another exciting sound which breaks the silence of the winter night is the strange scream of the fox hoping to find a mate. The fox is common on the fell sides, preferring the rocky fissures and natural hollows in the block screes. It feeds nearer to home on beetles and voles. The cubs' first lesson is on how to listen and pounce. The abundant shrews are caught, but left as unpalatable.

On the rough grassland of the slopes, sheeps' fescue and bent grass offer the best feed for sheep. The pale wiry *Nardus* (mat grass) is inedible and where competing grasses are reduced by over grazing it tends to take over the shallow slopes. Rushes grow in the wet areas. Bracken has invaded the fells to a worrying extent over the last century. While it gives the fells the lovely yellow and brown colours beloved of landscape photographers in the autumn, it is useless as feed, and poisonous to cattle if they develop a taste for it. Why the increase? One theory is that when cattle used to be allowed on to the fell sides, their trampling in the early spring, when the first tentative clock-spring-like shoots appear, would have been an effective control. Dry bracken is sometimes collected in the autumn for cattle bedding.

The yellow hammer may be seen around the bracken slopes, but the bird of the grassland is the meadow pipit; its nest is often chosen as a free nursery by the cuckoo. At these levels the blackbird gives way to the ring ouzel where he shares rock heaps and drystone walls with the wheatear and the pied wagtail. In the screes and by almost every rock grows the mountain parsley fern, its bright green almost translucent in spring. It is more abundant here than anywhere else in Britain. Bilberry, also growing around the rocks, offers some refreshment to hot fell walkers.

In the hollows and the ravines and about the old mine workings lives the ubiquitous tiny wren; its loud and lovely song amplified by the rocks. It is well named in Latin – *Troglodytes*, the cave dweller. The grey wagtail shares its habitat too.

On moorland in the Skiddaw and Silurian Slates live the golden plovers, but only where they are not disturbed. By drystone walls in some of these areas lives the merlin, the thrush-sized raptor. It flies low and relies on speed and manoeuvrability to catch its prey. The larger hen harrier, also localized in similar habitats, flies slowly with occasional glides, relying on a sudden drop to prey on the ground. In the Borders it is sometimes called the mouse hawk. Where there is a cover on the moor side of young conifers the short-eared owl also hunts for voles, often in daylight.

Some of the lower fell-side pools and bogs, which sometimes offer traps for unwary fell walkers in mist, have bog asphodel present, sometimes cotton grass and locally the bogbean. Some patches of boggy areas glow red with sundew, the fascinating little plant which gets its nitrogen from insects it captures, and digests, on its leaves covered with gluey red hairs. In the same area may also sometimes be found the butterwort, like bright green starfish. They catch their insect meals on their sticky green leaves which curl over to digest.

Some fell sides carry acres of juniper, sometimes climbing up the crag sides. It could be mistaken at a distance for gorse. Juniper is our only cypress. ('Savin' is its local name.) Its charcoal was much valued at the gunpowder mills at Elterwater and Backbarrow, but it has a more familiar use – its berries flavour gin. It is declining in other parts of Britain, but is a good survivor in the Lake District – sometimes colonized by long-tailed tits and linnets.

Does the buzzard belong to the fells, or the

Beech woodland (National Trust) at Calf Close Bay by Derwent Water.

lowlands? Really it belongs to the air, for what finer sight is there than that effortless flight, wheeling and turning in the air currents and thermals? Its haunting mewing cry is evocative of the wild places. They are as happy nesting at 1,500 feet as in lowland woods. The buzzards lost ground when they were severely persecuted by gamekeepers; and later they suffered from the pesticide menace. But they have gained in numbers. They are often mistaken for eagles but they lack the heavier head and beak, and the feather trousers.

The fells offer great long-term prospects for the naturalist explorer. He will not be concerned so much with the head down, best foot forward, keep to the paths approach. He will linger and look and listen and wander by the green places and the gullies and mark the bird passage and twists of the crag-side tree. To him the fells then take a deeper meaning: they are no longer just large muscle-stretching open-air gymnasiums, but part of the great web of life in which all belong. He will not be concerned with mere peak bagging. He will probably also not be half as wet and tired.

Broad-leaved woodlands have drastically declined over the last three decades – at least half of them have gone from all over Britain. Modern economic philosophy favours the short-term profit from quick growing conifer plantings. Time has gone when the landowner planted good hardwood timber trees for his grandchildren and great grandchildren. Back to medieval times, if not beyond, the broad-leaved woodlands were maintained. Regular cropping by coppicing (felling and allowing the stumps to produce new shoots) perpetuated tree cover. It was sensible management. No one now has time for it. In the Lake District National Park plantations and larger woodlands cover some 10.7 per cent of the area, with a little less than half of them broad-leaved. It is fortunate. The National Trust owns and preserves around 5,000 acres of broad-leaved woodland, and plants an area with about 50,000 trees each year. The national park has acquired several key woodlands and manages others to a total of 1,000 acres. The Forestry Commission's policy is to preserve the broad-leaved areas in its ownership (ten per cent of Grizedale Forest's 8,715 acres). Planting grants are available to landowners.

Broad-leaved woodlands, whether historically under constant tree cover, as some are in the south of the national park, or man-made plantations, are

The buzzard. Commonly seen in typically effortless, soaring flight in many parts of the Lake District.

Wood anemone, a typical woodland plant.

Green woodpecker.

usually on land unsuitable for agriculture, such as steep rocky slopes with outcrops. From an aesthetic, and the naturalist's, viewpoint, this makes them varied and interesting. The commonest woodlands, as from the earliest times, are of sessile oak (with stalkless leaves and acorns) and birch. Birch is the great colonizer, quickly invading abandoned quarries. In the wet areas quick-growing alder is abundant. The mixed woodlands typically have an understorey of hazel. A feature of the Lake District woods is the abundance of mosses and liverworts. Some of the woods on acid soil are designated as sites of special scientific interest because of this and are internationally important. Indeed, some woods in Borrowdale are unique.

Typical woodland ground cover, depending on drainage and amount of light, might be bluebells, wood anemones, wood sorrel, wavy hair grass, primroses, foxgloves, meadowsweet and ransomes; but there are always some surprises.

Hopefully some dead trees are left standing. If so all three native woodpeckers are then present; the lesser-spotted being less seen as they live high, though they come to some bird tables in winter. The woodlands of early summer are loud with the dawn chorus of wood warbler, chaffinch, red start, pied flycatcher, blue, great and coal tit, wren and robin, often in the background the raucous call of the carrion crow. If the birdwatcher is clumsy he will be spotted by a jay which will raise Cain. A quiet observer may well enjoy watching the gravity-defying tree creepers or a nuthatch.

In the limestone woods ash predominates with hazel and the ground cover, apart from dog's mercury, might include some orchids, herb paris, and lily of the valley, and some shrubs. This is an area favoured by whitethroats, garden warblers, and marsh tits. Amenity woods with some conifers might attract our smallest bird, the goldcrest, as well as blackbirds and siskins.

The commercial forests of conifers are relatively poor in flora and fauna. At their early stages however they produce a burst of activity. A dramatic rise in the number of voles often results. They could damage the young trees severely but invariably the predators move in. One such is the little owl, usually nesting in a wall hole.

In the south of the national park and at Thirlmere there are herds of red deer. The woodland breed is heavier than its fell cousin of Martindale. A binocular view of a mature stag at rutting time,

Roebuck in summer.

indignant from hearing a distant challenge, mud-caked from his wallow, his great head of antlers decorated with tree branch fragments – that is something to remember.

The beautiful smaller roe deer has increased its population and its range over the last few decades. They often move around in small family groups at early dawn and dusk. Residents in the Windermere and Keswick areas find them in their gardens if they have not fenced them off. They devastate the roses. Alas, many are road casualties and some are cruelly poached to serve the ready market for venison. Some fawns are killed by well intentioned people who find them lying in bracken and think that they have been abandoned and pick them up. The doe purposely hides her scentless fawn and leaves so that predators cannot find it through *her* scent, returning at intervals to feed it. Once a fawn bears the human scent its mother cannot recognize it and abandons it.

The Lake District is one of the remaining English habitats of the red squirrel. Populations

A young red squirrel.

unaccountably rise and fall. Ideally they need a mixture of oak, hazel and conifers and some of their habitats have gone. Large gardens are favoured, and some come to bird tables in winter. They are handsomer, and far less destructive, than their grey squirrel cousins which were introduced from America. There are no greys in the national park though they are very near. If they were to invade, the red squirrel would decline. Red squirrels too are frequent road casualties. So are the badgers which have also increased in numbers.

There is concern about the possible effects of acid rain on British woodlands. There is no evidence that it has had any effect on trees in the Lake District. The worst period for acid rain must have been late last century and early this century when Lancashire's mills were in full smoke, but there is no direct evidence of damage then. The first threat would be to some of the lichens which are sensitive to air pollution; but observations do not go back far enough to judge any effect. Records available to the Freshwater Biological Association on the acidity of tarns and lakes, coupled with recent research, shows that there has been *no* increase in acidity in the last thirty-five years in the tarns, or for fifty-six

Middle reaches of the River Duddon.

Grasmere.

years in the lakes.

Water makes an interesting study and there is a lot of it in the Lake District. The habitats it provides are tremendously varied. Following a water-course from its boggy source on the fell, by beck down its falls to and through the lake, and then by river to the sea, together with its environs, could take a lifetime of research. A short chapter must leave much untold.

Where lively young streams plummet down the rock animal life is sparse. Only creatures which have adapted to strong currents, by offering little bulk resistance – like flatworms – or which have attachments for hanging on to stones – like the nymphs of *Ecdyonuridae* (mayfly) – can survive.

Downstream life is increased with the addition of molluscs and insect larvae, and examining the underside of a stone from the bed with a $10 \times$ lens will reveal this surprising little world. The quiet beck-side observer might see the tiny predator, the water shrew, a treat to watch as it appears to be wearing sequins – its fur traps air bubbles. As the beck gains in volume there is that amazing bird the dipper, which walks underwater using the force of the current on its wings and back to hold itself down. Its lovely song sounds suitably liquid. A pool is likely to be guarded by a motionless heron, ready to stab any small trout imprudent enough to break the surface.

The amount of life in a tarn or lake depends upon its purity. Wast Water and Ennerdale Water, for instance, fed straight off the fells, are very pure, and offer little in the way of nutrients to sustain animal life. At the other extreme Esthwaite Water and Rydal Water, relatively shallow with a long beck running into them through agricultural land and human settlement, are 'eutrophic' – not polluted, but rich in base minerals. Most lakes are in between the extremes. Examination under stones in the shallows will very probably reveal the freshwater shrimp; and *Asellus*, the water-living relative of the wood louse. Undersides of stones when looked at through the magnifier will reveal small blobs which will expand as they move and show themselves as small leeches and flatworms. There will be tiny snails, and perhaps caddis, mayfly, or stonefly larvae, perhaps a tiny red mite. This is near the bottom, not only of the lake, but of the food chain. Above it are the minnows, trout, perch, pike, and eels. The char, a deepwater trout living in Windermere but also in other deep lakes, cannot survive in temperatures above 60°F (15°C). Potted Windermere char was a great delicacy on gentlemen's tables early last century. Its stripes and hump-back identify the plentiful perch. The biggest might reach up to a foot long. Much bigger are the pike, a 'freshwater shark' at the upper end of the food chain.

Char.

There are two rare fish. In Ullswater, Red Tarn on Helvellyn, and Haweswater is the Schelly, sometimes thought of as a freshwater herring; it is silver, moves in shoals, but is no relation. It was once caught for food in large numbers on Ullswater by the placing of a net across the lake's narrowest point: hence the name of the northern promontory, 'Skelly Neb'. The other rare fish found only in Bassenthwaite Lake and Derwent Water, is the Vendace, similar in form to the Schelly, but with a pointed head.

Water fowl are plentiful about the lakes. The white-headed coots (hence 'as bald as a coot'), locally great crested grebe and little grebe breed regularly. Of the ducks, mallard are numerous, sometimes holding up traffic as they march their chicks across minor roads to the water; and in winter even scrounging scraps on the lakeside village pavements. Tufted duck, teal, merganser, goosander and mute swans also breed by the lakes, and sandpipers haunt the lake edges. Winter tourists are numerous. Whooper swans are a welcome sight, often using Elterwater (Old Norse name for 'lake of the swans') but their numbers have declined. Goldeneye, pochard, widgeon, shovellers and cormorants make their annual appearance, and sometimes the divers: great northern, red throated, and black throated. Greylags and Canada geese graze the lake shore grass.

Otters are now a rare sight where they were once common. The reasons for their absence might be complex; certainly disturbance would be a major factor, though a holt recently was made in a fairly public place. Mink, from an earlier release from a mink farm, have increased and are widespread, but not to the extent that had been feared.

Down river the dipper might be around again, maybe with a nest under a bridge. Hopefully, but less likely for some unknown reason now, there will be a kingfisher. The swamps and mosses and reed beds might have reed buntings, sedge and grasshopper warblers, snipe and lapwing; and in the still night might be heard the strange 'churring', or the 'jarring' of the nightjar, one of the strangest of all birds, the ghostly insect feeder with the silent moth-like flight.

The dipper, on its stone perch in its beck territory. The bird has mastered the art of walking underwater, even in swift currents, to turn over stones in search of food.

9 The national park yesterday and today

The Lake District National Park Authority (official title 'The Lake District Special Planning Board') was once accused by an irate person of being 'a neo-fascist para-military junta'. One could assume that he was not very pleased at being told what he could not do in a national park. Rules are often thought to be made by faceless autocrats.

The National Park Authority, in true democratic

Nature conservation (National Park Plan Review 1986).

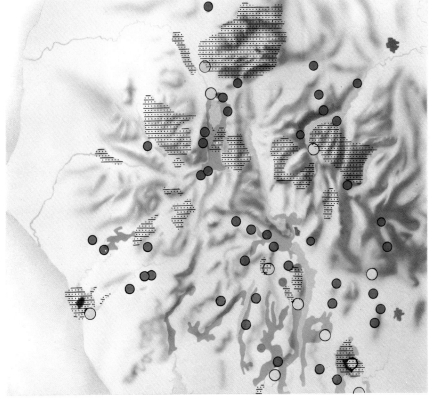

Broad-leaved woodland zones	◯ Cumbria Trust for Nature Conservation Reserves	● National Nature Reserves
Sites of special scientific interest areas	● Sites of special scientific interest	■ Local nature reserves

National Trust campsite
screened by trees.

tradition, is administered by a Board. It consists of
sixteen County Councillors, who are appointed by
Cumbria County Council every four years, and four
District Councillors who are elected annually; and
ten members appointed by the Secretary of State, on
advice from the Countryside Commission, who
serve for at least three years. It is funded by a grant
from the Department of the Environment, and one
from the County Council, and has an income from
trading. The proportion has been about fifty, twenty
and thirty per cent.

The authority's main duty is to preserve the
landscape and it has full planning powers within the
park. Any development (with one or two exceptions
for agriculture and forestry) which will have some
impact on the landscape, no matter how small, is
subject to control. Over a thousand planning
applications are dealt with each year.

The measure of success in planning control is *not*
what one can see; but what one *cannot* see. There is
still 'not a single red tile' or 'gentlemen's flaring
house' to ruin the view of Grasmere. (But thankfully
now no 'happy poverty'.) There are no new hotels
or caravan sites on the shores of Bassenthwaite – or
Windermere. There are no great building spreads
beyond the existing village boundaries. The
buildings which have been allowed cannot be seen
because architecturally, and by the use of traditional
building materials, they merge into the existing
scene. Perhaps the more sensitive can wince at what
might be judged to be mistakes; and that
independent body, the Friends of the Lake District,
is an effective watch-dog with a very loud bark; but
on the whole the authority has been successful
enough to earn national and even international

approval.

In the same cause of landscape preservation the authority can make Tree Preservation Orders, and can arrange for grants to be made for tree planting schemes. It can deploy staff and volunteers where necessary to repair erosion and wear and tear caused by visitor damage to property. Its ranger service can call upon many volunteers and its anti-litter team to keep the area tidy. It has a commitment to liaise with the agricultural and forestry interests which can make a dramatic impact on the landscape.

A major attraction of the Lake District landscape lies in its extremely diverse natural habitats. Organizations concerned with nature conservation were active from the beginning in the promotion of national parks, and obviously the protection of the park's flora and fauna must be a continuing major concern. Indeed if public access might come into conflict with a sensitive habitat, conservation must take priority; though in fact such issues are rare. What is so encouraging is the extent of public sympathy and awareness. As an instance, when climbers have been asked to avoid a particular 'pitch' on a climbing crag because of nesting birds they have readily responded. Indeed climbers sometimes advise the national park rangers on the location of nest sites and have co-operated on 'guard' duties of sites subject to robbery.

Many, though by no means all, of the important areas in need of care in the park are listed by the Nature Conservancy Council as Sites of Special Scientific Interest. In 1986, at a time when the Conservancy Council was reviewing needs (under the requirements of the 1981 Wildlife and Countryside Act) there were sixty-eight sites listed and four National Nature Reserves. There were also thirteen other reserves, eleven of them in the care of the voluntary body, The Cumbria Trust for Nature Conservation. The National Park Authority must obviously support the statutory and voluntary bodies in the protection of sites; but it must also have a special care for all those areas not receiving special recognition but which are, none the less, part of the vital natural scene.

The Lake District Planning Board Order of 1951 created the National Park Authority and it lost no time in tackling the problems which had been outstanding for years, including outdoor advertising and above-ground power cables. Its success is now taken for granted.

In the interests of preserving the landscape and

for making contact with the visiting public it created its first voluntary wardens in 1954 who immediately made some effort to remove the worst of the litter which had been accumulating in some places for many years; and in 1960 it created its first full-time warden, expanding the service in future years. In 1964 the first anti-litter team was formed to control the litter black spots and to remove old rubbish tips. In the first year, with volunteer help, it removed over sixty tons.

The first big test for the national park came by way of the promotion of the Manchester Corporation Water Act 1965, which provided for the abstraction of water from Windermere and Ullswater with the works that go with it, and the construction of a pipeline down Longsleddale. In the long term there was also a proposal to flood part of the beautiful Winster Valley, to the south east of Windermere. There was at once a great feeling of outrage from locals and visitors. In its opposition to the scheme the National Park Authority had tremendous support, including voices in both Houses of Parliament, with Lord Birkett, the distinguished advocate, as main spokesman. At the public inquiry arguments against the scheme were marshalled

An angler at Ullswater.

effectively. The Minister however felt compelled to decide that Manchester needed the water from Ullswater and Windermere. However, the scheme was radically modified. There would be *no* development in Longsleddale; buildings and structures would be subject to very stringent planning needs. Water extraction should be limited and controlled by physical barriers. The opinion of the Minister, too, was that Manchester should look elsewhere if it needed further water in the future. Only in theory was the national park's case lost. In practice its opposition with so much support had a salutary effect. No works are visible at all at Windermere or Ullswater and no one could possibly know that water was being abstracted, for straining wells and pumps are completely underground. With abstraction limitations there are no bleached shore lines which are a scarring feature around normal reservoirs. Even in the long drought of 1984 the lakes were not excessively low.

The next big fight was lost. The authority had agreed that west Cumbrian industry needed a better road from Penrith and the M6 than the existing one through Keswick. However, when the plans were produced in 1970 they included very extensive new road works on the A66 with a large viaduct over the scenic Greta Gorge, and works built into the shore line of Bassenthwaite Lake. In opposing the scheme the authority suggested the the route should be sited outside the park following existing roads from Penrith to Cockermouth. Although just over four miles longer it had advantages of easier gradients and access to other Cumbrian towns. Again enormous support was enjoyed, much gathered by the Countryside Commission and the Friends of the Lake District. The enquiry lasted for six weeks and there was confidence that a cast-iron case had been made. The decision then that the scheme should go ahead was received with astonishment, and a motion by Lord Henley 'to call attention to the decision' and for an 'urgent need to look at road policy for the National Park' was supported by the Peers; but the Secretary of State refused to review his decision. The bulldozers were on the move.

One concession was won later. It was argued successfully that since the A66 was designed to move industrial traffic from the M6 at Penrith, there was no need for heavy vehicles to go through the centre of the park via Windermere, Ambleside and Keswick (on the A591). A ban on such traffic was

Wast Water, with Wast Water Screes behind.

agreed and appropriate signs placed on the M6. Probably one small compensation too is that the park has acquired the length of abandoned railway line through the beautiful Greta Gorge below and out of sight of the A66 until the viaduct is reached, and has made it a pleasant path.

The next threat came in 1978. The North West Water Authority proposed to increase water abstraction from Ennerdale Water by raising its level and lowering an extraction point. At the same time, British Nuclear Fuels Ltd, who were already taking four million gallons of water each day from Wast Water, proposed to increase the abstraction to eleven million, raising the level with a new weir. The proposals were met with general disbelief. The national park objected to both schemes and suggested that, as an alternative, water should be taken from the River Derwent. The subsequent inquiry lasted for fifty-seven days in 1980 and feelings were running very high. In the event the Secretary of State decided *not* to allow increased abstraction from either Ennerdale or Wast Water. BNFL were given temporary permission to increase its abstraction from Wast Water by fifty per cent until it got its alternative source. Perhaps at last it

Brockhole, the National Park Visitor Centre.

A lane at Troutbeck.

was beginning to be realized that the majority of the public feels that national parks should be inviolable.

What next? Whatever, the national park must be ready to meet the challenge.

In the future the park intends that more resources should be directed towards improving the landscape. But it has also a duty to help the public to enjoy the amenities, and to do so the authority has its Information Service, with centres in the main villages. It produces information leaflets and sells maps and books. In the late 1960s the authority acquired Brockhole, a large house, gardens and grounds on the shores of Windermere between Ambleside and Windermere town, which had been a convalescent home. In 1969 it was opened as the country's first National Park Visitor Centre, with walk-through displays, lecture theatre, cafe and shop. The gardens were preserved as they were planned by the original nineteenth-century owner. It could not have been better placed. Annual visits now exceed 135,000.

The authority also has a Youth and Schools Liaison Service maintaining contact with education authorities, schools, and outdoor pursuits centres. In the closer field contact with visitors, particularly at weekends and holiday times, it has the ranger service and the corps of 300 voluntary wardens. Guided walks and courses for the public are organized.

Meanwhile, the land within the park continues to be farmed as it has for centuries.

Lakeland farming, by modern standards, is like its traditional 'Herdwick' breed of sheep: old fashioned, relatively small; but come storm, come freeze an incredible survivor. Some of the farming families have been in the business for many generations, which is one explanation of why it endures: no prudent 'offcomer' would consider buying in on such marginal farming. The best land is on the lower fringe areas, but in agricultural terms that is only Grade 3 (with moderate constraints, usable mainly for dairy produce and some cereals). The best hill farm 'inbye' land – valley bottom and close to the farm – is usually barely Grade 4. A second reason for survival is that the National Trust owns some eighty-six farms in the region, and is dedicated to their preservation, even if in modern terms they are not viable. The Trust owns 22,500 sheep which are let to its tenants, for the sheep go with the farms. The sheep are predominantly small Herdwicks. Founder Canon Rawnsley, and Beatrix Potter who gifted farms to the Trust, wanted the breed preserved, and they do well on the Lake District fells. Swaledale-Herdwick crosses are favoured by many farmers.

The typical fell farmer works to a routine little modified from that of long ago. Lambs are born from the middle of April. At the end of May they are put on the fell with the ewes. In June, weather permitting, haymaking will start. July is dipping time, then on until August, clipping. The lamb sales are in September, ewe sales in October, when it is dipping time again. For the winter feed, blocks are put out on the fells, sometimes by pony, sometimes a group of farmers will combine to hire a helicopter. Supplementary feeding continues.

Hill farmers have always kept a few cattle. In earlier days the breeds of Galloway, Blue-grey, Highland and their crosses roamed the fells; their trampling prevented the encroachment of bracken. Nowadays farmers tend to keep Friesian and Hereford cross beasts, the Continental breeds also being introduced. They are more productive but being less hardy make demands on the lusher, lower 'inbye' land, and the inedible bracken spreads further on the fell slopes.

Shepherd and walkers near Hartsop.

What is extraordinary is the tolerance that the farmer has for the problems caused by visitors to the national park. Some supplement their income by catering for them. Sometimes the problems get exaggerated but on the whole the scores of minor irritations are shrugged off, and the average farmer and his family can even find time to exchange conversation and answer visitors' questions. The big problem is uncontrolled dogs. Dogs that savage sheep are not common; but the pet dog which chases for fun, or out of curiosity, can at best upset the grazing pattern so that vital feed is lost; at worst cause a ewe to drown in a beck or a ewe in lamb to miscarry. A farmer can shoot an offending dog and the owners can be fined. Some farmers would say that as dog lovers they would be happier shooting the owner and fining the dog; for some dog owners seem to act irresponsibly. Under the Wildlife and Countryside Act 1981 it is an offence to have a dog, not under control, in enclosed land containing sheep, even though it might not be interested in sheep.

One can be reassured by a visit to a Dales show when the farmers gather to show off their stock and have a 'crack' with their mates, and maybe have 'a bit of a stir'. Little apparently has changed. The same faces and cheery groups enjoy the great annual social event. Distant cousins, aunts and uncles, meet and exchange news. There are keen comments on the sheep breed standards.

The facts are though that the family farms are diminishing in number. Since 1963 over a quarter of the farms have gone. Ministry of Agriculture census figures in 1981 show that although the Lake District farms employed some 2,800 people, the number of farms had diminished. The decline is thought to be continuing by about seventy a year. Between 1975 and 1981 the figures show that 142 family farms, and 104 part-time farms were lost. The trend has been for several smallholdings to be run as one. While this might make for a viable unit, in landscape terms the result can be serious. It might mean more fences and a deterioration in drystone walls and hedges, perhaps the removal of some. A study sponsored by the Friends of the Lake District in four parishes (Borrowdale, Ireby, Longsleddale, and the South Winster Valley) in 1985 has shown that since 1947 thirty-seven miles of walls have gone and dereliction has increased. The loss of hedgerows was worse – seventy-seven miles. There was an increase in fencing – a third of the boundaries. Here is scope for the national park to start to help to remedy this deterioration.

There are other causes for concern. While labour is scarcer EEC sheep subsidies have encouraged farmers to increase their stock. Between 1975 and 1981 sheep and lamb numbers grew by thirteen per cent to 734,986. Overgrazing has always been a cause of landscape deterioration. In public, farm spokesmen will not admit that it exists. In private they might guardedly admit that there is 'some'. When sheep eat out their grazing area they stray on to someone else's. This does not help good neighbourly relations, and with the impossibility of the former regular shepherding, there is pressure for fells to be fenced. The National Park Authority has to resist this on landscape and access grounds.

Another problem has no easy solution. When a farm comes on the market there is a tendency to break it into lots to attract a higher price. This often means that the farmhouse becomes a retirement home or a holiday cottage, and there is pressure to convert other redundant farm buildings. The boundaries of the fields, which are acquired by a distant farm, are fenced and the walls neglected. But more important – another farming family has gone.

Perhaps children are lost to the village school and the decline in numbers might mean its closure. The village shop will suffer.

The National Park Authority must do all it can to support hill farming. Already it has undertaken, without cost to the farmer, to replace stiles and gates worn out by visitors. It will help to repair broken walls and grant aid tree planting, or arrange for the planting to be done by park staff. It can consider anything within its statutory powers.

There are long-term worries. If the farmers of the productive lowlands of Britain are tempted by EEC policy to move from grain growing to sheep rearing, the hill farmer could never compete. The price of hill land for farming is falling. But there is a demand for land for forestry, and private concerns are eager to buy units even as small as 100 acres. If this happens to any extent the traditional landscape could dramatically change.

The Forestry Commission will admit that there might be increasing pressure by private forestry concerns to buy marginal land. Forestry is not subject to planning control, an anomaly that has long concerned national park authorities and amenity groups. However, the safeguard is that the Forestry Commission has an obligation to consult the

Good forestry management in a National Trust wood at Calf Close Bay, Derwent Water, showing their programmed felling of mature conifers and fenced planting of hardwoods.

planning authority and the Countryside Commission before giving planting grants, and the system has worked. But if a private concern was tempted by low land prices and tax incentives to buy bare land and plant without a grant, the Forestry Commission would have no control.

The major Lake District forestry controversies came before the establishment of the national park. There was bitterness when the Forestry Commission bought 7,000 acres of fell land in Dunnerdale and Eskdale in 1935 and planted conifers in spite of great public protest. Out of the controversy grew an agreement between the Commission and the Council for the (then) Preservation of Rural England that 300 square miles of the central Lake District should not be planted. The agreement has served its purpose for fifty years.

In recent times the Forestry Commission has been more sensitive to public opinion. They have embarked on a programme of thinning and varying the straight lines of their enclosures which have marred the landscape for so long, for instance at Thornthwaite Forest above Whinlatter, and Bassenthwaite, and in Ennerdale.

In 1985, following a concern about the savage loss of native broad-leaved trees (over forty per cent nationwide since 1947), often to be replaced by alien conifers, the Commission launched a new policy for broad-leaved woodlands: to enhance the old woodlands and promote and encourage new planting.

In the 1960s the Commission noticeably changed their policy of discouraging public access to their plantations to actually encouraging it. The Lake District's Grizedale Forest was a pioneer in this, opening a museum and visitor centre in the early 1960s. Many thousands enjoy woodland walks. If the Commission's holdings are sold off would the new owners be as accommodating?

The pressure for the introduction of national parks and access to the hills, which gathered its momentum between the wars, came from walkers and climbers. The National Parks Act secured that 'freedom of the hills' and, in the words of the Hobhouse Committee which introduced the Act, 'There must be free access for ramblers on the mountains and moorlands and country sports and pursuits should be made available to all who find in them a source of health and refreshment – a new sense of adventure'. There is no true wilderness in

Climbers consult a climbers' guide-book *en route* to Gimmer Crag in Langdale.

Britain. The fells of the Lake District are the nearest that one can get to it. Walking and climbing among them can offer the ideal opportunity for adventure and a sense of freedom; and those who need solitude can find it there, even at the busiest holiday time.

Fell walking is now more popular than ever. It is not impossible to stand on a fell in the Yorkshire Dales National Park and look across to the Lake District hills over twenty miles away and see the footpaths. In the past fifteen years up to 1986, footpath erosion on the fells has greatly accelerated. Erosion is easily started. The soil is thin and acid and is a poor supporter of vegetation. It is also subject to winter's frost and thaw and the heavy rainfall. The poor grass that is pounded by boots is soon destroyed without a chance of recovery. A groove is worn that becomes a channel in rainstorms. There is a wash-out. Walking on the path becomes unpleasant so new paths start either side of the old and *they* erode and become unpleasant, so the instability spreads. A disheartened national park ranger said of his patch 'If this keeps up the grooves will get so deep that we might consider roofing them and turning them into a cave system'.

There is no slick and easy solution to the erosion problem. There are hundreds of miles of it on the fells. Some of the worst fell-side examples are being repaired by the National Trust and the national park with the help of Manpower Services and the British Trust for Conservation Volunteers.

Rock climbing as a sport could be said to have begun with the pioneer achievements of a barrister, Walter Parry Haskett Smith. In 1886 he made the first, solo, ascent of Napes Needle on Great Gable. Other early climbs in the nineteenth century were on Scafell Crag, Pavey Ark, Pillar Rock, and Dow Crag, Coniston. Since then the Lake District has produced hundreds of high-grade climbs. The most popular areas are Langdale, Borrowdale, Coniston, Thirlmere; but climbs have been pioneered in more remote areas, and climbing guide-books proliferate. There is an enormous growth in the sport, and climbing techniques have reached a stage, with the modern equipment, undreamed of two decades ago. The sport too has been much fostered by education authorities and outdoor pursuits centres. Some of the approaches to the climbing crags, and the summit evacuation routes, as well as some of the scramble routes, are also

Reconstruction work on
an eroded fell footpath.

becoming well worn.

The wear and tear is an indication of the
enormous growth in popularity of the hill sports. It is
a good healthy activity. It is freedom and challenge
with a spice of adventure. Adventure implies an
element of risk. The Mountain Rescue Teams now
turn out over 200 times each year for incidents
involving injury, death, and missing persons. The
teams are all volunteers. The park helps with capital
grants and the teams have the support of the ranger
service; but much has to be done by rangers, youth
and school liaison officers and the Information
Service to educate walkers on safety: about the right
equipment; careful planning; and the vast
differences between conditions on the fell and in the
valley. The park's 'phone in' weather forecast is a
help (Windermere 5151). This is supplemented by a
report on fell-top conditions supplied by the ranger
service in the winter.

The Lake District National Park is the supreme
walking area of the country with over 1,500 miles of
public rights of way and many thousands of acres of
open country. Walking does not necessarily mean
strenuous climbs up the fells because most of the
footpaths, and much of the open country, are at low

levels. Since 1979 the authority has acted as agents of the Highway Authority in taking over responsibility for public paths. By 1990 it is intended that a programme to sign all rights of way at the points where they leave the public roads will be completed. (Over 1,600 signs were still needed in 1985.) A programme of path maintenance and improvement follows a yard-by-yard survey of all the paths by the ranger service in 1986. Even this job has to be done with some delicacy. No one wants to see paved paths in the countryside. The only exception should be those provided for the use of the disabled – a long neglected concern.

The lakes themselves also provide recreational opportunities and enjoyment for visitors.

Following complaints, the owner of a fast power boat was asked to leave Esthwaite Water, where power boats of any kind are not permitted. He remarked 'What a pity. I was enjoying myself here. It's such a quiet lake'. The Hobhouse Committee in its report stated that 'people need the refreshment which is obtainable from the beauty and *quietness* of unspoilt country . . . .

Freedom is the essence of countryside recreation: but the individual's share has to be

Lake District lakes offer a variety of opportunities for leisure activities.

The round-the-lake boat
service on Derwent
Water.

limited to the extent that he will not be a nuisance to
others.

Quietness is getting increasingly difficult to find.
Many come to unspoilt country with the expectation
of enjoying it. Where else but a national park? And
in it where else but when walking or sitting by a lake
shore? After a programme of consultations the
National Park Authority submitted proposed by-
laws to the Secretary of State prohibiting the use of
the smaller lakes for power boating. These were
approved in 1974. By-laws coming into effect later
placed speed limits on Coniston Water and Derwent
Water of ten miles per hour, coming into effect too
on Ullswater in 1983 when it was hoped that power
boat owners, particularly water-skiers, would have
found some other venue for their sport. The
introduction of the by-law was opposed by power
boat lobbies and some tradespeople. The final effect
was heartily approved by local inhabitants and by
Ullswater's regular visitors.

As anticipated, the by-laws have increased the
pressures on Windermere, the largest lake, where
every form of water activity takes place – often all at
the same time. A by-law was introduced to compel
all owners of power boats of any kind to register

their crafts. By 1985, some 20,000 boat owners from all over Britain were licensed. The importance of registration is that the police, and the traffic wardens employed by the District Council (who own the bed of the lake) can identify offenders.

Negotiations over many years for the opening of Thirlmere, which is a reservoir, for sailing craft and canoes, came to fruition at last when the Water Authority's new treatment works came on stream. After two trial periods, in 1983 and 1984, it was decided to allow the access to continue.

The great increase in lake usage everywhere has come from canoeists and also from wind surfers. Both sports are quiet and wholly in keeping with national park values. One problem with wind surfing is that it is so easy to lift and carry the craft, that they are appearing on the less accessible lakes. Some might like to see multi-coloured sails on Grasmere. Others might find them as offensive as a red-tiled roof.

Over the last few centuries people have fled to the Lake District to escape the blight and the chaos and the worries of the man-made; to capture, if only half fearfully, half unknowingly, through the limitations of their Claude glasses or the modern equivalents,

Blea Tarn, Langdale, owned by the National Trust, with the Langdale Pikes behind.

something of the purity and truth of the uncorrupted countryside.

The essence of the great scene is the harmony of the elements; the balance. Caring for the huge national park scene is a balancing act – there are so many demands being made by so many self-interested people.

It is so easy to regard the park as a mass of problems. The task is to produce that harmony out of some discord. Harmony implies a co-operation, a mutual support. Given that, the mass of problems become a wealth of opportunities.

Those who care all have their part to play.

Selected places of interest

The numbers after each place-name are the map grid references to help readers locate the places mentioned. Ordnance Survey maps include instructions in the use of these grid references.

The Lakes

Boat launching is permitted on Thirlmere, Coniston Water, Derwent Water, Ullswater, and Windermere at approved places. Power boating is allowed only on the latter three. Only on Windermere where registration is needed are speeds allowed over 10 mph .

Swimming. Lake water is very cold. Even in a heat wave cold currents can be met. Generally the lakes are dangerous for non-swimmers owing to deep holes in the lake beds, and shelving.

Fishing. A Water Board rod licence is required. Enquire locally for permits.

BASSENTHWAITE LAKE (NY 20 26) 4 miles long by $\frac{1}{2}$ mile wide 51 ft (15.3 m) deep. Owned by National Park. Enjoyment somewhat marred by noise from A66 from which there is some shore line access. Best walkers' access from Mirehouse (permit required from Forestry car park NY 235281). Visit the house if open!

BROTHERS WATER (NY 40 12). Small lake at the northern foot of Kirkstone Pass. Public footpath on western shore.

BUTTERMERE (NY 17 15) (National Trust) $1\frac{1}{4}$ mile long. A lake of superb beauty, changing colours, dramatic backcloth. Possible to walk right round it on public and permissive paths.

CONISTON WATER (SD 29 90) 5 miles long. 145 ft (44 m) deep. Scene of fatal attempt by Donald Campbell to break water speed record. Historical steamboat 'Gondola' (National Trust) plies the lake. Boat hire at landings (SD 308970) (National Park). Lovely quiet public path along the west shore at Torver Back Common (National Park). Brantwood, Ruskin's home, is on eastern shore.

CRUMMOCK WATER (NY 15 17) (National Trust) Buttermere's larger 5 miles long neighbour, 144 ft (44 m) deep. Impressive rather than beautiful. Best views from hills above the road.

DERWENT WATER (NY 25 19) Keswick's lovely and popular lake. Only 72 ft (22 m) deep. Good shore line walking on National Trust land on west, linked with piers served with helpful regular motor launch service from Keswick landings. Many viewpoints. One of the best and easiest, Friar's Crag, south of boat landings.

ELTER WATER (NY 33 04) Small pretty lake taking the waters from the Langdales before decanting them down Skelwith waterfalls. Public path on the east and northern side.

ENNERDALE WATER (NY 09 14) An out-of-the-way $2\frac{1}{2}$ miles long lake – a reservoir really but not too noticeably so. Lovely walks from Forestry Commission's car park NY 110153. It is possible to walk round the lake – takes longer than you think.

ESTHWAITE WATER (SD 35 95) A lovely little lake by Hawkshead. Wordsworth spent happy schooldays here. Car park (National Park) and shore access at SD 362954 soon fills with anglers.

GRASMERE (NY 33 06) Wordsworth's lake, what else? Good shore line views from Penny Rock woods (National Park) (NY 343061) and on south and west shore (National Trust). Classic viewpoint is from Loughrigg Terrace on southern side. Boat hire near village.

HAWESWATER (NY 47 11) A 3½ mile long reservoir made from a smaller lake dammed in the '30s which drowned the settlement of Mardale. Only access to shore as yet on western side.

LOWESWATER (NY 12 21) (National Trust) A pretty little lake with outflow going into Crummock. Limited access by road side. Path on the western side.

RYDAL WATER (NY 35 06) Wordsworth's last thirty-five years spent close by this little lake. Public path on southern shore linking with Loughrigg Terrace and Grasmere.

THIRLMERE (NY 30 13) A 3½ miles long reservoir dammed and flooded by Manchester Corporation in 1894, settlements drowned in process. Agreement between Water Authority and park secured access in the 1980s. It is possible now to walk along much of the western shore and on the north-eastern. Light craft launch at Armboth. No swimming.

ULLSWATER (NY 39 16) the second largest lake. 7½ miles long, somewhat serpentine. Helvellyn range at south. An admirable motor yacht service on the lake, and a popular excursion is to take the boat it from Glenridding to Howtown and to return on foot by lake shore and terrace paths. Many viewpoints.

WAST WATER (NY 14 04) England's deepest lake. The towering Wast Water Screes on the south-east side plunge down from 2,000 ft (610 m) to the lake bed a further 250 ft (76 m)

below. Bed is 200 ft (61 m) below sea level. View along the lake to its head takes in the big fells – Kirk Fell, Great Gable, and the Scafells.

WINDERMERE (SD & NY 37 SD 86) England's largest 10½ miles long lake, 219 ft (67 m) deep in the upper basin. No less beautiful for its great popularity. A 'steamer' service plies its length. Scores of great viewpoints: eg Adelaide Hill near Bowness (SD 403986) (National Trust). Public paths on western shore.

Some principal fells

Words of advice: Strong footwear, waterproofs/windproofs, large-scale map and compass (and know how to use them) are necessary. In planning, a good rule to follow (assuming reasonable fitness): calculate walking at 3 miles per hour, add half an hour for each 1,000 feet of ascent. (Or 4 km per hour plus 10 m of ascent per minute).

BLACK COMBE (SD 135855) 1,857 ft (600 m) Neglected by walkers because of its remoteness. Wordsworth justifiably enthused about its view – central fells and Isle of Man, maybe Wales.

BLENCATHRA (Saddleback) (NY 323277) 2,847 ft (868 m) A true mountain in every sense best seen from St Johns in the Vale. Easiest ascent from car park by Blencathra Centre (NY 302257) Intrepid fell walkers via Scales and by Sharp Edge above Scales Tarn.

BOW FELL (NY 245065) 2,960 ft (902 m). Towers above upper Langdale among the billows of central fells. Main approach is from Stool End (NY 277057) and the Band.

CONISTON OLD MAN (SD 272978) 2,631 ft (802 m). A large range scarred by quarries old and new and riddled with old mine holes. Usual approach from Coniston village and the fell gate (SD 289970) and north and west by Low Water; a better way is by Walna Scar, then north west by Goats Water. Superb views.

FAIRFIELD (NY 359118) 2,863 ft (873 m). Ambleside's fell – but a long walk and very treacherous summit in mist. Usual start by Rydal and Nab Scar, descending by High Pike to Sweden Bridge.

GREAT GABLE (NY 211104) 2,949 ft (899 m). 'Great' indeed! Best seen from Wasdale, but best climbed from Seathwaite in Borrowdale (NY 235123) or (cheating from a height gain) from Honister Pass summit car park. The popular rock climbs are at Napes on the eastern flank (including Napes Needle).

HELVELLYN (NY 342152) 3,118 ft (950 m). Most climbed mountain in England. In fact a large range from Dollywaggon Pike in the south to Great Dodd. Most popular approach from Glenridding via Striding Edge (National Park) or by Swirral Edge, good routes. Treacherous for the unwary between November and May. Ice axes needed in snow. Other routes are from the car parks on the Thirlmere side.

HIGH STREET (NY 441110) 11 miles long ridge along which goes a Roman road (hence name). Shepherds used to meet on summit to swap strays, drink ale and race horses.

LANGDALE PIKES Now usually means Harrison Stickle (NY 282074) 2,415 ft (736 m); and Pike of Stickle (NY 275074) 2,323 ft (708 m): magnificent twins seen from so many viewpoints. The pikes actually include Pavey Ark, Thorn and Loft Crags. Usual routes to them all are from Langdale car parks (National Park & National Trust) (NY 295064) by Stickle Tarn or west via Mark Gate.

SCAFELL (NY 208065) Not to be confused with Scafell Pike next door. Most impressive feature below the 3,162 ft (964 m) summit, is the great cliff, 984 ft (300 m), on its northern side where serious rock climbing

was born. Most popular ascent of the fell is from the base of the crags and by a groove: Lord's Rake. Erosion means that this should now be classed as a rock climber's route. An ascent by Burnmoor Tarn is relatively easy, but tedious. A fine approach, though long, is by Eskdale to the south and by Slight Side. There is *no* direct access for walkers from Scafell to Scafell Pike. If it is to be reached the safest way is via Foxes Tarn to the east.

SCAFELL PIKE (NY 216072) 3,210 ft (978 m). The highest point in England. The fell would be as popular as Helvellyn but many give up, or get lost, part way. The summit is confusing in fog. Shortest ascent route is east from the head of Wast Water by Brown Tongue, then either south east by Mickledore, or north east by Lingmell Col. The long, most rewarding way is from Seathwaite in Borrowdale, via Styhead and south by the Corridor route (not in mist though). Note, there is *no* direct route for walkers from the Pike to Scafell.

SKIDDAW (NY 261291) 3,053 ft (931 m). Keswick's monster mountain, not rough and few crags. The usual 'no problem' ascent is by the side of Latrigg and by the old bridleway beloved of Victorian tourists; rewarding except on a hot day. Views from summit and from Carl Side to the south-west are unchallengable – lakes and central fells to the south, Isle of Man west, Scotland north.

Principal villages

AMBLESIDE (NY 37 04) A largely Victorian town built to provide for the tourists. Ideally placed for walking and touring. Walkers can limber up on the two close-by fells, Loughrigg and Wansfell Pike. Stock Ghyll Waterfall east of village. Oldest house Bridge House over River Rothay. Photo gallery and lecture theatre 'Photoscope' in the Slack. Nearby Waterhead for the boats, steamer pier. National Park Information Centre in car park. Also by Waterhead, Borrans Field, site of Roman fort, Galava.

BOWNESS & WINDERMERE (SD 40 96) The honeypot but yet *not* of the worst commercial kind. Bowness Bay for boat hire, steamer pier, and the promenade on which is the National Park Information Centre and Theatre. Steamboat Museum at the north-west end has some historical lake vessels carefully restored. Railway finishes at Windermere village. Best viewpoint over all is above the village at Orrest Head (SD 414994). $1\frac{1}{2}$ miles towards Ambleside is the National Park Visitor Centre, Brockhole. Here is the National Park's permanent walk-through exhibition, lectures, films, café, garden to lake shore. Ideally everyone should make it an early call.

BROUGHTON IN FURNESS (SD 213875) Unspoilt friendly village, once an important market town. Market square has character. A National Park conservation village. Museum contains vintage motorcycles.

CONISTON (SD 30 97) Good walking and touring centre. National Park Information Centre and the Ruskin Museum in the main street. Boat landings (National Park) and steamer pier to south east.

GRASMERE (NY 337074) Wordsworth of course. His old home Dove Cottage and the fine museum at Town End (NY 342070). Wordsworth graves in churchyard. Good popular walking centre for Langdale, Helvellyn, and delectable places. National Park Information Centre west of the church.

HAWKSHEAD (SD 352981) A pretty village of timber-framed houses dating from when this was an important market. The grammar school where Wordsworth was schooled is by the church. National Park Information Centre opposite. 3 miles to the south west is Grizedale Forest's Visitor Centre and famous 'Theatre in the Forest' (SD 336944).

KESWICK (NY 26 23) Popular northern walking and touring centre. It has everything one can enjoy within reach: lake and Borrowdale, radiant in spring and autumn. A galaxy of viewpoints above and around. Museum by Fitz Park. Cumberland Pencil Museum reveals a town's old industry. National Park Information Centre at the Moot Hall in town centre.

RAVENGLASS (SD 084964) Once a busy little port. Base for 'Laal Ratty', the Ravenglass and Eskdale narrow gauge steam railway which once carried ore and granite, now passengers $5\frac{1}{2}$ miles to Elysian Eskdale. Roman fort invisible but Walls Castle Roman Bath-House to south east (SD 088959). Muncaster Castle and its lovely gardens $1\frac{1}{4}$ miles east.

Glossary

beck – stream
bield – sheltered or protected land, or refuge
brant – steep
cairn – heap of stones
cams – stones capping a drystone wall
dale – valley
dub – deep pool in a beck
fell – hill or mountain
force – waterfall
gate – street
ghyll or *gill* – watercourse in a ravine
gimmer – sheep aged between first and second shearings
hause – summit of narrow pass
heft – flock of sheep holding a defined fell area
Herdwick – local unique breed of sheep
hogg – a young sheep not yet reached first shearing
holme – island
how – rounded hill
inbye land – enclosed land close to a farm
intake – enclosed land claimed from a fell above the inbye
knott – rocky outcrop
nab or *neb* – promontory
pike – sharp summit
rigg – ridge
savin – juniper
seaves – rushes
scar – escarpment
scree – loose rock debris
slape – slippery
stint – defined grazing area
swill – local basket woven from strips of oak
tarn – small lake, usually high-level
thwaite – clearing
tuff – hard volcanic rock used to make Neolithic stone axes
tup – ram
twinter – sheep 'two winters' old
wether – castrated ram
yat – gate
yow – ewe

Bibliography

Brunskill, R W, *Vernacular Architecture of the Lake Counties*, Faber, 1974.

Clare, T, *Archaeological Sites of the Lake District*, Moorland, 1981.

Davies, Hunter, *The Good Guide to the Lakes*, Forster Davies, 1984.

Duerden, F, *Best Walks in the Lake District*, Constable, 1986. (Mixed-level walks.)

Hervey, G A K, and Barnes, J A G, *Natural History of the Lake District*, Warne, 1970.

Marshall, J D, and Davies-Shiel, M, *Industrial Archaeology of the Lake Counties*, Moon, 1977.

Millward, R, and Robinson, A, *The Lake District*, Eyre Methuen, 1974.

Murdoch, J, (ed), *The Lake District: A sort of national property*, Countryside Commission / V & A Museum, 1986.

Nicholson, N, *The Lake District: An Anthology*, Penguin, 1978.

Nicholson, Norman, *The Lakers; the Adventures of the First Tourists*, Hale, 1972.

Parker, J, *Cumbria; a Guide to the Lake District & its County*, Bartholomew, 1977.

Parker, J, *Walk the Lakes; 40 Easy Walks*, Bartholomew, 1983. (Low-level walks.)

Parker, J, *Walk the Lakes Again; 38 Easy Walks*, Bartholomew, 1985, (Low-level walks.)

Pearsall, W H, and Pennington W, *The Lake District; A Landscape History*, Collins, 1973.

Pevsner, W, *Buildings of England: Cumberland & Westmorland*, Penguin, 1970.

Pevsner, W, *Buildings of England: North Lancashire*, Penguin, 1969.

Postlethwaite, J, *Mines and Mining in the English Lake District*, (1877) reprint Moon, 1975.

Poucher, W A, *The Lakeland Peaks*, Constable, 1960.

Rollinson, W, *History of Cumberland and Westmorland*, Phillimore, 1978.

Rollinson, W, *A History of Man in the Lake District*, Dent, 1967.

Rollinson, W, *Life and Tradition in the Lake District*, Dalesman, 1981.

Sands, R, *The Wordsworth Country*, Hale, 1984.

Shackleton, E H, *Geological Excursions in Lakeland*, Dalesman, 1975.

Taylor-Page, J, *A Field Guide to the Lake District*, Dalesman, 1985.

Victoria and Albert Museum, *The Discovery of the Lake District*, V & A Museum, 1984. (Exhibition catalogue.)

Wainwright, A, *A Pictorial Guide to the Lakeland Fells*, 8 vols, Westmorland Gazette, 1955–74.

Wordsworth, William, *Guide to the Lakes*, (1810) reprint Oxford university Press, 1973.

In addition large-scale maps are essential for the proper and safe exploration of the area. The Bartholomew's one-inch-to-the-mile map is suitable for touring; the Ordnance Survey Tourist Map of the same scale carries more detail and both cover most of the national park. Much greater detail is in the four Ordnance Survey Outdoor Leisure Maps of two-and-a-half inches to the mile (1:25,000).

The national park also produces a number of publications on the Lake District. A list of these can be obtained from the National Park Information Officer; publications for teachers can be obtained from the Youth and Schools Liaison Service (both based at Brockhole in Windermere).

Useful addresses

British Trust for Conservation
  Volunteers,
National Park Visitor Centre,
Brockhole,
Windermere,
Cumbria LA23 1LJ
(Tel: Windermere (09662) 3098)

Council for National Parks,
45 Shelton Street,
London WC2 9HJ
(Tel: (01) 240 3603)

Countryside Commission,
Northern Regional Office,
Warwick House,
Grantham Road,
Newcastle upon Tyne NE2 1QF
(Tel: (091) 232 8252)

Cumbria Trust for Nature
  Conservation,
Badger's Paw,
Church Street,
Ambleside,
Cumbria LA22 OBU
(Tel: Ambleside (0966) 32476)

Cumbria Tourist Board,
Ashleigh,
Windermere,
Cumbria LA23 2AQ
(Tel: Windermere (09662) 4444)

Forestry Commission,
Grizedale Forest,
Hawkshead,
Ambleside,
Cumbria LA22 OQJ
(Tel: Satterthwaite (022) 984 373)

Friends of the Lake District,
Gowan Knott,
Kendal Road,
Staveley,
Kendal,
Cumbria LA8 9LP
(Tel: Kendal (0539) 821201)

Information Officer and Youth and
  Schools Liaison Service,
Lake District National Park Visitor Centre,
Brockhole,
Windermere,
Cumbria LA23 1LJ
(Tel: Windermere (09662) 6601)

Lake District Special Planning Board,
Busher Walk,
Kendal,
Cumbria LA9 4RH
(Tel: Kendal (0539) 24555)

National Trust,
Rothay Holme,
Rothay Rd,
Ambleside,
Cumbria LA22 OEJ
(Tel: Ambleside (0966) 33883)

Youth Hostels Association,
Church Street,
Windermere,
Cumbria LA23 1AV
(Tel: Windermere (09662) 2301)

INDEX

Page numbers in *italics* refer to illustrations.